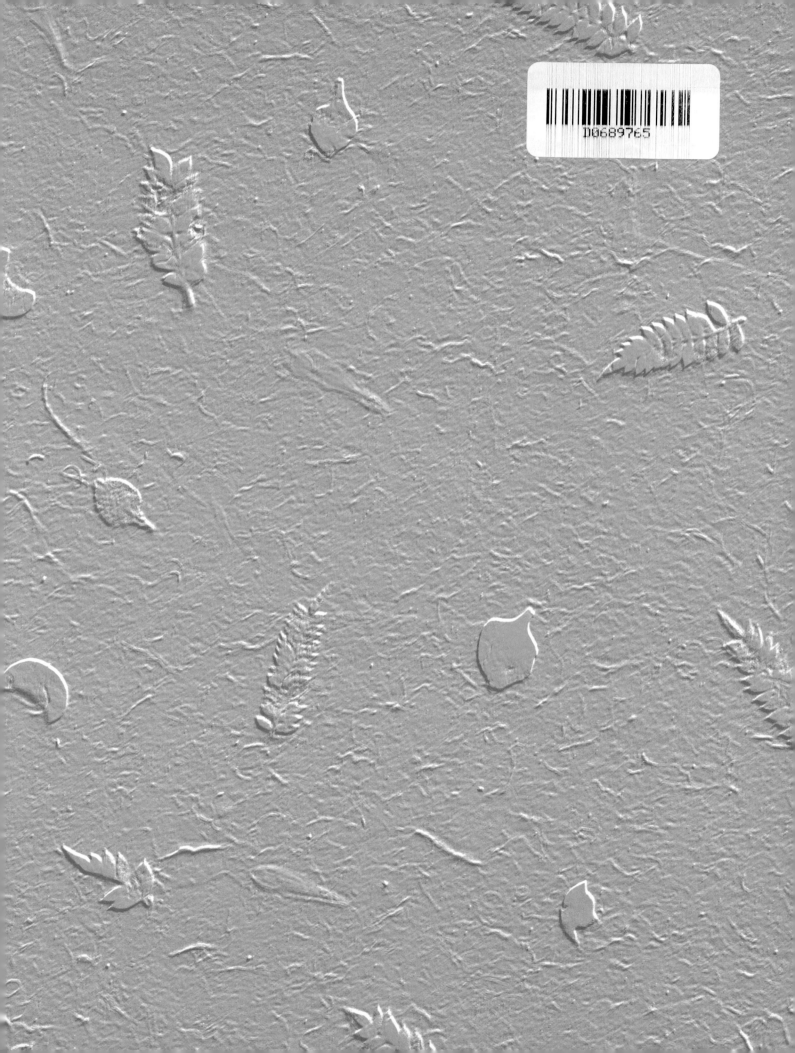

Creative Scrapbooking

Over 300 Cutouts, Patterns & Ideas to Embellish & Enhance Your Treasured Memories

by Sandi Genovese

HUNTING FOR CHESTNUTS

Sterling Publishing Co., Inc. New York

A Sterling/Chapelle Book

For Chapelle Limited
Owner: Jo Packham
Editor: Ann Bear

Staff: Marie Barber, Areta Bingham, Kass Burchett, Rebecca Christensen, Dana Durney, Holly Fuller, Marilyn Goff, Holly Hollingsworth, Shawn Hsu, Susan Jorgensen, Pauline Locke, Barbara Milburn, Linda Orton, Karmen Quinney, Leslie Ridenour, Cindy Stoeckl

Photography: Kevin Dilley, Photographer for Hazen Photography

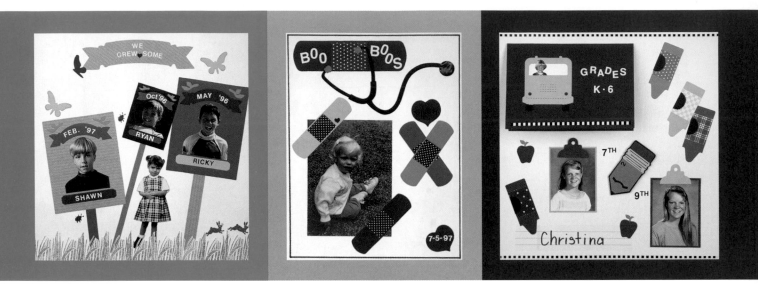

Library of Congress Cataloging-in-Publication Data

Genovese, Sandi.
    Creative scrapbooking : over 300 cutouts, patterns
& ideas to embellish & enhance your treasured
memories / by Sandi Genovese.
      p.   cm.
    "A Sterling/Chapelle book."
    On t.p. : Ellison.
    Includes index.
    ISBN 0-8069-5913-4
    1. Photograph albums.   2. Photographs--
Conservation and restoration.   3. Scrapbooks.
I. Ellison Craft & Design. II. Title.
TR465.G47   1999   98-43774
745.593--dc21   CIP

10 9 8 7 6 5 4 3 2 1

Published by Sterling Publishing Company, Inc.
387 Park Avenue South, New York, N.Y. 10016
© 1999 by Chapelle Limited
Distributed in Canada by Sterling Publishing
c/o Canadian Manda Group, One Atlantic Avenue, Suite 105
Toronto, Ontario, Canada M6K 3E7
Distributed in Great Britain and Europe by Cassell PLC
Wellington House, 125 Strand, London WC2R 0BB, England
Distributed in Australia by Capricorn Link (Australia) Pty Ltd.
P.O. Box 6651, Baulkham Hills, Business Centre, NSW 2153, Australia
Printed in United States
All rights reserved

Sterling ISBN 0-8069-5913-4

If you have any questions or comments, please contact:

Chapelle, Ltd.
P.O. Box 9252
Ogden, UT 84409

(801) 621-2777 • Fax (801) 621-2788
chapelle1@aol.com

Sandi Genovese
Senior Vice President and Creative Director,
Ellison Craft & Design

Sandi Genovese is a multitalented artist, author, and educator who serves as the idea generator at Ellison® Craft & Design, "The Idea Company." She is the diva of die-cuts — coming up with creative new ways in which teachers and crafters can use the Ellison® Letter-Machine™, then demonstrating her techniques through videos, workshops, and television appearances.

She also gives scrapbook enthusiasts many innovative ideas on how to make their scrapbook pages come alive through her book *Memories in Minutes* — a definitive how-to book on designing scrapbooks.

Sandi taught school for eight years, then served as a curriculum specialist in the Newport Mesa School District in California. There, she helped teachers come up with creative ways to teach. That is also where she got her first taste of Ellison products — she purchased an Ellison LetterMachine for her school district.

As Sandi found new ways to use the machine in her district, she passed the innovation on to Bob and LaDorna Eichenberg, Ellison's founders. Ellison soon hired Sandi to write and illustrate their newsletter, which contained ideas on using the Ellison LetterMachine.

In 1985, Sandi came to work at Ellison full time as an artist and LaDorna Eichenberg's assistant. She became Senior Vice President in 1994. Today, her duties include serving as the creative director for Ellison, overseeing art direction, pioneering product development, producing videos, and writing books and articles on Ellison products. Sandi still designs new dies and ways to use them. In fact, many new developments in the die-cut industry — including using perforation to denote detail on cutouts — are the brainchild of Sandi or LaDorna. She still finds time to talk with teachers and crafters regularly, listening to their ideas and suggestions. Clients will tell you that Sandi is one of the reasons Ellison is a preferred choice company. Sandi travels internationally, giving workshops on how to use die-cuts to enhance personal scrapbooks and other craft projects. She saw possibilities for the Ellison LetterMachine beyond paper — developing ways to use it for rubber stamping, sponge painting, stenciling, and more — and she is always willing to teach her techniques to others. On television, she has shown thousands of viewers how to make their projects more memorable. Her appearances include *Good Morning America*, *For Your Home*, *Carol Duval Show*, *Home and Family*, and *The View*. She has written articles and created projects for numerous publications, including *Creating Keepsakes, Good Housekeeping Do It Yourself*, and *Craftrends*.

Table of Contents

General Instructions

Scrapbooking has never been easier than with *Creative Scrapbooking*. Whether you are a first-time scrapbooking enthusiast or have been scrapbooking for years, this book will boost your creativity and polish your skills. *Creative Scrapbooking* includes simple techniques as well as more advanced projects.

Before you begin, it helps to keep a few basics in mind. The most important element to begin with is the photo! All of the other elements are decorative to help the photos tell a story or come to life. Do not allow the decorative elements to contradict or overwhelm the photos.

Begin by selecting the photos you want to save in your scrapbook. Think thematically. Separate the photos that logically go together on the same page or double-page spread. The theme should coordinate with the photos you have chosen. Select cutouts, stickers, and other decorative features that would enhance the theme of the scrapbook page(s).

Place the photos, cutouts, and stickers on the page, being mindful of basic design principles, such as color, placement, and balance. Know when to stop! Do not crowd your page with too many elements.

Move the photos and cutouts around the page until the design is pleasing before adhering them to the page. Yes, it is that easy!

Tip: Have all of your supplies in order before you begin, and give yourself lots of choices. For example, if your photos are vacation shots taken at the beach, there may be twenty different cutouts that are beach related. Try them all. Use the extras on other pages and every page is certain to be easier.

General Project Steps

The following steps apply to all projects in *Creative Scrapbooking*:

1. Read all General Instructions for techniques, materials, and tools. Each project also has a specific list of cutouts, materials, and tools.

2. Copy or trace and transfer specific Cutout Patterns from pages 100–120 onto assorted papers.

3. Affix mounting adhesive sheets on the back of assorted papers before cutting. Mounting adhesive sheets can also be mounted behind photos or photo copies.

4. Cut all cutouts from assorted papers.

5. Refer to individual project photo as a guide for the placement of photos, cutouts, and embellishments on cutouts and scrapbook page.

Photographs

Photo Tips

Creating a special scrapbook begins with photos. Before planning or attending a special event, think about how the photos can be used to re-create that event. Keep these objectives in mind as photos are taken. Select backgrounds that will provide the right atmosphere for the event. Make certain close-ups are taken of people (subjects) involved. Limit the number of scenery photos. Sometimes it is helpful to have a person in the photo to provide scale for the scenery.

Select your best photos for the scrapbook. "Best" may mean the most colorful, most candid, a special accomplishment, event, or subject. The size and number of photos placed on a scrapbook page depends on the size of the pages and how much cropping is done to each photo. Photos can be further enhanced by matting them on complementary colored paper.

Use a red-eye remover pen to remove red eyes from photos. There are separate pens available for people and pet photos.

Color Photocopies

A good rule of thumb is to print two sets of the photos, one for your scrapbook and one to keep in a photo-safe box. If you have only one set of prints, color photocopies are a great solution. Any photo can be replaced on your scrapbook page with a color photocopy to allow for preservation of original photo for framing or storing. If you have not seen color photocopies lately, you are in for a real surprise — they look great! Most copy centers have color photocopy machines and a machine that can make a print from a print. Make certain the paper in the color copier is acid-free. If you are concerned about photocopies being acid-free, cover the page with a plastic sleeve or place in a photo holder. Color photocopies provide freedom to experiment with photos on the page. If you do not like the result, make another copy. The same photo can be used several times to

Photo corners may be purchased or handmade, using Decorative or Plain Photo Corners on page 114.

create a memory album for each member of your family or friends. Enjoy the photo now and save the original for the future. Color copies may also be used to enlarge or reduce a photo size.

Even if a photo is sepia toned or black and white, it is important to use a color copier. A color copier will pick up all shades of brown or gray in the photo, while a black-and-white copier will only reproduce in black and white. Reproductions from a color copier do not have as grainy a quality as those made with a black-and-white copier.

Be mindful when photocopying professional photos, such as wedding photos and family portraits. Most are copyrighted by the photographer and can only be reproduced with permission.

Whenever possible, include dates and names on the page with photos. Anyone viewing the albums in years to come, will find it very helpful. Phrases can be added as reminders of a particular person or event. If possible, have the people in these photos write somewhere on a page or two. Their handwriting will become a precious memory.

Cropping a Photo

Cropping (cutting) a photo is an optional, yet sometimes effective technique that can draw attention to the page. Some examples of cropping include removing background or unwanted parts from a photo, trimming edges, creating a motif, or focusing on a primary subject. Cropping around a subject can make the photo more life-like. Among discarded photos may be other images or backgrounds to crop and use to enhance the scrapbook page. Photos can be cropped into motifs fitting the page theme, such as hearts or stars. Cropping can be done with scissors, paper cutter, or paper trimmer. Decoupage scissors are a must for detailed or curved areas.

Envelopes, Memorabilia Pockets & Photo Holders

Envelopes

Envelopes can be made from the *Gift Card with Insert* Cutout Pattern found on page 109, or purchased from a craft store. An envelope die-cut can be used in place of the envelope cutout, if desired. When making an envelope, choose a type and design of paper that enhances the look of the page.

Memorabilia Pockets

Memorabilia pockets are clear envelopes used to display souvenirs, such as baby hair, dried flowers, or baby teeth. A clear page protector is a good material for making a memorabilia pocket. They are also available at most craft stores.

Photo Holders

Use purchased photo holders if you want to protect only the photo and do not want to cover the entire page with a page protector. Photo holders come in a variety of sizes to fit standard size photos, and are self-adhesive, making it easy to attach them to the scrapbook page. Photo holders also can be used as memorabilia pockets.

Photo Corners

Photo corners come in a variety of colors (including clear) and have an adhesive backing. For best results, slide photos into corners before mounting on the scrapbook page. Photos are removable.

Hand-cut photo corners allow for a wider variety of materials. Many cutouts can be substituted for photo corners. Mount only a part of the cutout on the scrapbook page, leaving the remainder of the cutout free to hold the photo.

Acid-free

A scrapbook is meant to be a lasting memory for several generations. For that reason, the importance of using acid-free supplies cannot be emphasized enough. Products with high acid content can become brittle and crumble with age. Placing products containing acid next to photos can cause photos to fade, yellow, or become discolored.

Acid-free supplies have an approximate pH of 7 (neutral) on the 0–14 acid to alkaline scale. Various products can be used to test the pH of supplies, as well as to neutralize acidic objects. An acid (pH) pen uses color to test acid content. A deacidification spray is used to neutralize the acid content of souvenir items, such as theater tickets and programs. Buffered paper also may be placed under an object that is not acid-free, preventing acid in an item from spreading.

For a scrapbook full of lasting memories, make certain all scrapbook pages, papers, adhesives, cutouts (die-cuts), pens, ink pads, and stickers purchased are labeled acid-free or photo safe.

An acid (pH) pen and deacidification spray are two ways of ensuring your scrapbook will last for years.

Mats

Mats can be used to contrast, frame, or highlight a cutout, photo, or title.

The following techniques apply to creating mats:

- For a single mat, cut a piece of contrasting colored paper slightly larger than cutout, photo, or title and adhere the mat to the back of the cutout, using a mounting adhesive sheet or glue stick.

- For multiple mats, follow the above technique for several different colored mats, graduating in size ¼" to ½". Draw a border around the outside edge of each mat, using a straightedge ruler and colored marking pens for added definition.

- For a strip mat or frame, cut colored paper into strips and adhere around cutout, photo, or title, using a mounting adhesive sheet or glue stick.

Tip: Do not overuse any technique. Use a variety of different techniques to display photos in your scrapbook.

Cutout Patterns

Each project described in *Creative Scrapbooking* comes with its own Cutout Patterns found on pages 100–120. If you do not wish to use the Cutout Patterns, die-cuts are an option. A list of Ellison® die-cuts is provided on page 127, which corresponds to the Cutout Patterns on pages 100–120. **Do not cut Cutout Patterns from book.** They may be traced onto tracing paper, then cut out to be used as a pattern, or photocopied at a copy center directly onto colored paper or lightweight cardstock. Cutout patterns given are an average size, but may be enlarged or reduced, using a photocopy machine, to suit individual projects. Many cutout patterns include dotted lines to use as guidelines for adding details in contrasting colors, or for scoring and folding.

Embellishing Cutouts

Transform a simple cutout into a finely detailed design. Embellishing can be as simple as cutting the stem off a green apple and placing it on a red apple, or placing a contrasting color behind the lights of a school bus.

The following techniques apply to embellishing cutouts:

- Add multiple layers of patterned or contrasting colored paper for more detail.

- Cut one cutout pattern from multiple colors and layer. Since the same cutout pattern is used to cut each color, contrasting parts will align perfectly.

- Add details with colored pens or pencils.

Materials & Tools

When preparing for your scrapbook page, have these basic materials and tools on hand:

Double-sided tape

Glue stick

Mounting adhesive sheets

Paper: lightweight paper or cardstock in assorted colors and patterns

Paper trimmer (optional)

Pencil

Photos

Scissors: craft and decoupage

Scrapbook pages

Straightedge ruler

Adhesives

There are many choices for adhesives available. Unless otherwise noted, *Creative Scrapbooking* utilizes glue sticks, and mounting adhesive sheets for all projects.

Embellishing cutouts is easy! Add contrasting colors and some finishing details and you're done!

Double-sided tape is a great alternative to mounting adhesive sheets. It comes in a roll like regular clear tape. An advantage of using double-sided tape is you cut only the amount you need for a cutout or photo. However, some double-sided tape does not have a peel-off shield to prevent one side from being exposed to dust particles or lint. There are several types of double-sided tape available. Be certain to purchase acid-free tape made especially for scrapbooking.

Foam dots are double-sided, self-adhesive dots about ¼" thick. They are used to add dimension to scrapbook pages. Apply foam dots on the back of photos and cutouts to make them literally lift right off the page.

Foam dots should not be used excessively. Consider them for album covers, on the first page of an album, or in albums with page spacers. With time, the foam dot shape may leave an undesirable imprint on photos, cutouts, or other adjacent scrapbook pages.

Glue sticks are inexpensive and easy to use. Remove cap, apply glue directly on cutout, and adhere the cutout to the scrapbook page. Glue sticks are useful for complete coverage or for adhering precut motifs and souvenirs to pages.

Mounting adhesive sheets are similar to double-sided tape and available in 8½" x 11" sheets. Cut a piece of the mounting adhesive sheet approximately the same size as cutout pattern. Adhere one side of mounting adhesive sheet on back of cutout pattern and cut the shape. For ease and convenience, a mounting adhesive sheet may be mounted on an entire sheet of cutouts before cutting.

Scrapbook glue is an adhesive made especially for scrapbooks and is stronger than glue stick adhesive. It is available at most craft stores, and may be more appropriate for some projects than mounting adhesive sheets or glue sticks.

Albums, Scrapbook Pages & Page Protectors

Albums (scrapbooks) come in a variety of styles and sizes. The most popular sizes are 8½" x 11" and 12" x 12". Select the album best suited for your needs.

Three-ring binder styles offer the ease of adding and removing scrapbook pages. Albums with posts can be opened to add or remove

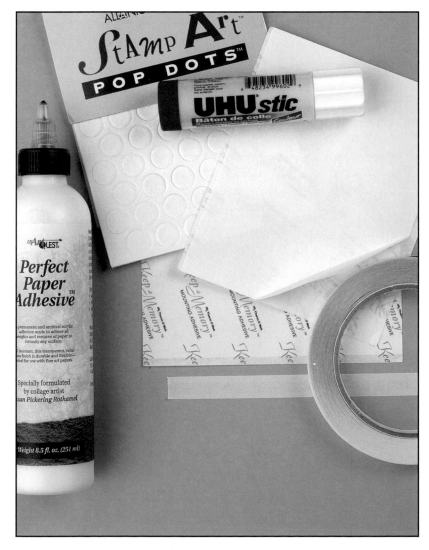

Scrapbook glue, foam dots, glue sticks, mounting adhesive sheets, and double-sided tape are only a few of the the many adhesive options available for scrapbooking.

When choosing an album or scrapbook page, consider theme as well as how the album pages will lay.

pages, but not as easily as a three-ring binder. There are albums with a set number of pages permanently attached. The page size of these albums are usually unique, making this style of album an excellent choice for commemorating that special event.

Scrapbook pages in some styles of albums lie flatter than in others when opened. Items that are fastened to flatter pages remain in better condition.

Page protectors are used to protect scrapbook pages from heavy use, especially by younger family members. Their function is to keep pages clean and to prevent an item, such as theater tickets or special memorabilia, from rubbing against other items on the facing page. However, photos lose some of their brightness and clarity when placed behind a page protector.

Scrapbook pages in some albums are actually page protectors with a background paper slid inside. Side or top loading page protectors are also available to slide onto regular scrapbook pages. Clear page protectors can be purchased for almost every style of album. Slide in your own choice of background paper.

Craft Punches

Craft punches generally provide a smaller version of a cutout for those times when tiny decorations are needed on the scrapbook page. Both positive and negative spaces may be used. They are available at craft stores and come in a variety of styles, shapes, and sizes.

One type of craft punch uses the palm of the hand or the thumb to apply pressure for cutting. Some craft punches resemble the traditional hand-held hole punch, with a decorative shape instead of a plain, round hole.

The corner rounder is another type of craft punch. It is used for rounding the corners of scrapbook pages and photos. Some corner rounders punch decorative elements in the corner of the page, and at the same time make a rounded corner.

Die-cuts & Die-cutting Machines

Die-cuts are precut shapes of paper or lightweight cardstock. All cutout patterns provided in *Creative Scrapbooking* are available in die-cuts. They are made by putting a die into a special press called a die-cutting machine along with the desired paper, cardstock, or clear page protector.

An endless variety of craft punches are available, which help to enhance scrapbook themes.

They are one of the easiest ways to decorate a scrapbook page and may be used to replace cutouts. Adhere die-cuts to the page, using a glue stick, or mount on pages with mounting adhesive sheets. It is easiest to mount adhesive to the paper first, then cut in die cutting machine. Some die-cuts come with a self-adhesive backing on them. Die-cuts are available at most craft stores and are sold individually or in theme packs.

Die-cuts may be used to create interactive pop-up pages. You may also use the negative portion of the die-cut to create unique frames.

Die-cutting machines are available for use in many craft stores. Stores generally do not charge to use the machines when you buy the paper or cardstock from the store. Also look for them in stationery stores, fine-arts stores, photo shops, and stores that sell rubber stamps. Die-cutting machines allow

Die-cuts are a great alternative to cutting by hand.

for creative control when cutting shapes and letters for scrapbook pages. These machines also can be used to emboss elegant features for scrapbook pages.

Using a die-cutting machine rather than buying precut die-cuts allows you more freedom of choice. You can cut as many of each design or letter as needed for your scrapbook. You can cut a wide assortment of products, such as maps from a vacation, theater programs, comic strips, wallpaper, self-adhesive paper, etc. You can even cut rubber for rubber stamps of your own design. Die-cut machines will cut anything scissors will cut, so fabric, felt, thin plastic, and other deco-

Die-cuts, stencils, and stickers are three ways of adding text to your scrapbook page.

rative elements can be added to your scrapbook pages.

Lettering & Pens

There are many ways to add titles or other text to scrapbook pages. *Creative Scrapbooking* offers two styles of alphabet and number cutouts, which are included with the Cutout Patterns on pages 100–120. Stencils, stamps, and stickers are other options and are available at most craft stores. Select the style and size of lettering that will enhance the photos and theme of the scrapbook page. Mix and match various types of lettering, depending on the image you wish to create.

Die-cut letters are larger and more commonly used for titles. Die-cut letters come in both upper and lower case in a variety of styles and sizes, or can be cut from your choice of materials, using an Ellison die-cut machine.

Calligraphy pens, paint pens, and gel pens add color and style with a personal touch.

Handwrite or print words directly onto the scrapbook page, using any number of specialty pens. It is easy to create a journal entry on a black or colored paper with a white, silver, or gold pen.

Calligraphy pens, colored markers, and felt pens not only come in many colors, but also with different styled tips. Some are used to add color to a page and others are specifically for lettering. There are even pens available with different tips at each end, allowing for creativity without changing pens.

Gel pens and paint pens make it easy to put any color print on top of any color scrapbook page. Use silver or gold ink on a red or black page for a dramatic effect.

Paper

Choices for paper have never been more vast. From handmade paper to colorful stationery, paper is available in an endless variety of colors, patterns, textures, and weights. Use these varieties to help create themes and moods.

Patterned paper, such as stationery or wrapping paper, is light- to medium-weight. It adds contrast or complements other decorative elements on the scrapbook page.

Textured paper is medium- to heavyweight, such as handmade, ruffle board, and linen, drawing the viewer's attention to the detail. Cardstock is light- to heavyweight and usually plain, making it an excellent choice for cards and card covers.

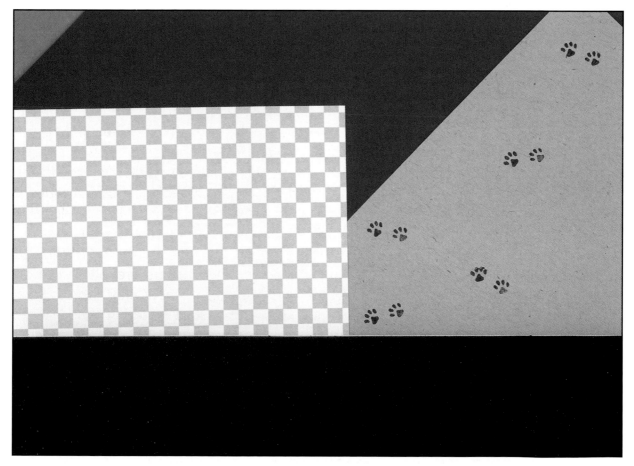

The right paper choice adds to the mood and theme of your scrapbook page. The paw print pattern on the paper above was made, using a rubber stamp.

Create an attractive border around a plain colored scrapbook page, using a combination of papers. It is especially important to accentuate photos with a colored mat, as you would a picture with a frame. Use patterned paper to enhance your scrapbook pages and to embellish the cutouts.

Paper Cutters, Scissors & Trimmers

Many craft stores have heavy-duty paper cutters for your use. Some are available with different blades for cutting decorative edges.

Craft scissors are used for cutting paper, light plastic, and other materials. Select a pair with comfortable handles to make scrapbook projects considerably easier.

Decorative-edged scissors are used to enhance the edges and corners of paper motifs, mats, and photos. The wide variety of edge patterns, from scallops to Victorian, make it difficult to choose just one pair!

Decoupage scissors are small scissors designed to cut awkward areas, such as detailed centers, intricate motifs, sharp angles, and curves.

Paper trimmers are used for cutting straight edges. They are a smaller version of paper cutters and are perfect for home use. Paper trimmers come in two types, a lever blade or a sliding, rotary blade.

Rubber Stamps, Sponges & Ink Pads

Rubber stamps provide another option for decorating scrapbook pages. They are easy to use and come in a wide variety of shapes and sizes, making it easy to find stamps to coordinate with the theme of the page. Decorate the image with felt pens after stamping, or emboss them with embossing powder and powder heating tools. It is also possible to make your own patterned paper, using tiny rubber stamps. Ink pads can be used with any traditional rubber stamp and come in every color of the rainbow.

Having the right cutters and scissors is a must. Paper will dull blades not designed for use with paper.

Stencils

Stencils come in every imaginable style and size, including lettering and borders. Stencils can be used to add color directly to the scrapbook page with colored pens, stencil paints, or used as templates to trace a shape for a cutout.

Stickers

Stickers add a decorative element to scrapbook pages. Stickers come in a wide variety of styles, covering a large assortment of themes. Use elegant stickers to decorate a wedding or anniversary page and whimsical designs for a child's birthday party. There are even stickers created specifically for use as scrapbook page borders, such as line stickers.

Rubber stamps and ink choices have never been more plentiful. Use them to enhance your scrapbook theme.

Stickers add instant color to pages.

Stencils are handy for borders, lettering, and embossing.

17

Chapter One
Simply Shapes

Cutouts are one of the easiest ways to decorate a scrapbook page. They can be moved around until the design is pleasing, then adhered to the page. There are hundreds of precut shapes from which to choose, or use Cutout Patterns provided on pages 100–120 and cut your own.

Cutouts can be randomly placed overlapping other shapes or over photos. Cutouts provide a simple and trouble-free way to add visual interest to your scrapbook pages.

The following steps apply when using Cutout Patterns:

1. Decide which cutout patterns will support the theme of the scrapbook page.

2. Do not cut patterns from the book. Use a copy machine and copy on desired paper. Enlarge or reduce as desired.

3. Cut patterns from photo copy. **Note:** If using mounting adhesive sheets, apply to back of copied patterns before cutting.

Boo Boos

In years to come, you and your children will enjoy looking back on childhood events, perhaps even tearful moments that accompany minor scrapes and spills. What better way to portray these moments than with bandages, a stethoscope, and a little TLC (heart).

Specific Materials & Tools

Cutout patterns: Bandage, Heart #2, Stethoscope
Shiny sliver paper
Permanent pen: black
Stickers: hearts, letters, numbers

Instructions

1-5. Follow steps in General Project Steps on page 6.

6. Embellish cutouts as shown.

7. Trace end of Stethoscope onto shiny silver paper and cut out. Adhere silver cutout to end of Stethoscope, using glue stick.

8. Adhere photo to page.

9. Mount cutouts on page.

10. Draw a line border around inside edges of page, using black pen and ruler.

"Let Mommy kiss it better."

WE GREW♥SOME

MAY '96

Oct '96

RYAN

RICKY

FEB. '97

SHAWN

20

We Grew Some

Specific Materials & Tools

Cutout patterns:	Banner, Seed Packets, Tiny Butterflies
Ink pads:	black, brown, green
Felt-tip pen:	red
Rubber stamps:	grass, ladybug, rabbit
Stickers:	hearts, letters, numbers

Instructions

1-5. Follow steps in General Project Steps on page 6.

6. Embellish cutouts as shown.

7. Cut posts from paper, using paper trimmer.

8. Crop photos.

9. Adhere a photo to each Seed Packet, using glue stick.

10. Mount posts, Banner, Seed Packets, and Tiny Butterflies on page. Adhere cropped photo to page.

11. Stamp grass on separate sheet of paper, using green ink pad. Cut grass from paper. Adhere grass to bottom of page.

12. Stamp rabbits on page, using brown ink pad.

13. Stamp ladybugs on page, using black ink pad. Color ladybugs, using red pen.

Hair Today, Gone Tomorrow

A haircut provides a terrific photo opportunity. It is fun to see the stages (before, during, and after) and the envelopes are a perfect format for doing just that.

Specific Materials & Tools

Cutout patterns:	Gift Card with Insert, Hair Dryer, Open 2D Envelope, Scissors
Page protector:	clear
Stickers:	letters

Instructions

1-5. Follow steps in General Project Steps on page 6.
Note: Do not apply mounting adhesive to envelope cutouts.

6. Embellish cutouts as shown.

7. Cut double mats for banners, using paper trimmer. Embellish banners as shown.

8. Adjust size of photos to fit envelopes, using a color photo copier. Crop photos, emphasizing the before, during, and after stages.

9. Make a memorabilia pocket from clear page protector, following instructions on page 61. Mount to page with double-sided tape.

10. Adhere envelopes to page, using glue stick. Do not adhere center openings of envelopes. Tuck photos inside envelopes and lock of hair into memorabilia pocket. Photos can be permanently adhered to envelope or left loose.

11. Mount cutouts on page.
Note: Banner and one envelope fit inside Scissors cutouts.

"What a cool idea for summer."

Splish Splash

Specific Materials & Tools

Cutout patterns: Beach Ball, Front Umbrella Diorama, letters, Snorkel,

Foam dots

Stickers: hearts, letters

Instructions

1-5. Follow steps in General Project Steps on page 6.

6. Embellish cutouts as shown.

7. Cut mats for photos, using paper trimmer. Adhere photos to mats, using glue stick. Mount mats on page.

8. Crop photos. Crop one photo to overlap Front Umbrella Diorama. Adhere photo behind frame, allowing part of photo to lay over top of frame. Mount frame on page. Mount remaining cropped photos on pages, using foam dots behind cropped photo.

9. Mount letters on page. Mount Beach Ball and Snorkel on pages, using foam dots.

10. Embellish page with heart and letter stickers.

ESTHER WILLIAMS

EAT YOUR ♥ OUT

Chapter Two
Wreaths

Wreaths are a perfect choice for the cover of a scrapbook or title page. They also provide a unique format for highlighting a special photo.

A wreath page can literally be a Christmas wreath encircling a holiday photo or can refer to any design that forms a wreath frame around the photo you wish to highlight. While traditional wreaths are circular, your wreath can be circular, rectangular, or square, depending on the photo and what will look best on the scrapbook page.

Cutouts can be mounted directly on the page around the photo; however, it is safer to create a ring or frame that acts as a structure. A ring provides the backbone to support and shape the wreath. This helps to keep the wreath symmetrical and prevent a lopsided wreath, and makes photo placement much easier.

The following wreath instructions apply to all projects in this chapter:

1. Cut a ¼"-wide frame in the appropriate shape for photo.

2. Arrange cutouts around frame. When pleased with arrangement, mount cutouts to frame with mounting adhesive sheets or glue stick.

3. Mount double-sided tape to back of frame.

Love

Specific Materials & Tools

Cutout patterns: assorted hearts, "Love"
Foam dots
Stickers: hearts, polka-dot border

Instructions

1-5. Follow steps in General Project Steps on page 6.

6. Embellish cutouts as shown.

7. Mount two small hearts on two large hearts, using foam dots.

8. Follow wreath instructions on page 27 to make wreath, using assorted heart cutouts.

9. Position photo behind wreath. Adhere to page, using glue stick.

10. Mount "Love" and small heart cutouts on page.

11. Embellish page with heart and polka-dot border stickers.

The following embossing techniques apply to projects in this chapter:

- **Die-cut machine embossing** may be done by sliding paper between a male and female embossing plate and pressing out the embossed shape.

- **Faux embossing** is a shortcut that adds the beauty of embossing without the extra time. Cut shapes from the same kind of paper as background page and adhere on the page in one or more layers with glue stick or mounting adhesive sheets.

- **Stencil embossing** is accomplished by using an embossing stencil, stylus, and light-table or sunlit window to make an impression on the backside of a piece of paper.

1. Lay stencil on front side of paper (or back side, depending upon which side will show the raised design) and lightly tape stencil to paper. Turn over so paper is on top of stencil and tape to a light-table.

2. Using stylus, press around edges of design from side to side or top to bottom. Gently but firmly press paper into stencil to create a raised design. Avoid scrubbing stylus across larger areas of design, as this may leave grooves in paper.

35

Wedding Invitation

Instructions

1-5. Follow steps in General Project Steps on page 6.
Note: Cut cutouts from same kind of paper as background page.

6. Adhere wedding invitation to page, using glue stick.

7. Mount cutouts around invitation, using faux embossing technique on page 35, or follow wreath instructions on page 27.

8. Embellish page with rose and silver border stickers.

Specific Materials & Tools

Cutout patterns: Bird #2A, assorted hearts
Stickers: roses, silver border

We have experienced love in
our parents, our families and friends,
and now a new love in each other.
With sincere joy and desire to give
this love its fullest expression
we will be joined in marriage
Saturday, August thirtieth
Nineteen hundred and ninety-seven
at seven o'clock in the evening
Heritage Park
Dana Point, California

Hors D'oeuvres Reception to follow
Decorative Arts Villa
San Juan Capistrano

We invite you to celebrate
our day with us

Kerry Bicknell & Sal DiPasquale

Congrats

Specific Materials & Tools

Cutout pattern: "Congrats"
Permanent Pen: black, silver
Stickers: roses, silver border

Instructions

1-5. Follow steps in General Project Steps on page 6.
Note: Cut cutout from same kind of paper as background page.

6. Cut a mat frame with appropriate-sized opening for photo. Draw a line border around outside edges of frame opening, using silver pen.

7. Position photo behind frame. Adhere to page, using glue stick.

8. Draw a line border around outside edges of frame, using black pen and ruler.

9. Mount "Congrats" above frame, using faux embossing technique on page 35.

10. Embellish page with rose and silver border stickers.

Photo reproduced with permission of Gina Chiaramonte, Photographer

Dad & Mom

Specific Materials & Tools

Old black and white photos were copied, using a color copy machine. Subtle colors were added, using colored pencils.

Cutout patterns: Banner, Bird #2A, Bird #4, Bookmark Heart, Butterfly, Heart #1A

Needle or pin
Permanent pen: blue
Ribbon: ¼"-wide grosgrain in coordinating color

Styrofoam sheet

Instructions

1-5. Follow steps in General Project Steps on page 6.
Note: Cut cutouts from same kind of paper as background page.

6. Place desired number of cutouts on styrofoam sheet. Poke holes in cutouts in desired pattern for a lacy appearance, using needle or pin.

7. Mount cutouts around photo, using faux embossing technique on page 35, or follow wreath instructions on page 27.

8. Position photo behind frame. Adhere to page, using glue stick.

9. Personalize Banner, using blue pen. Mount Banner on page.

10. Cut ribbon into strips to fit around edges of page. Adhere ribbon strips to page.

joseph & Sarah

Grandpa & Grandma

Instructions

1-2. Follow steps 1 and 5 in General Project Steps on page 6.

3. Emboss dot pattern on a sheet of paper, using die-cut machine embossing or stencil embossing technique on page 35. Trim right edge of paper, using decorative-edged scissors.

4. Adhere embossed paper to page, using glue stick.

5. Cut paper into nine ⅛" x ½" strips, using paper trimmer. Align and adhere strips to left side of embossed paper to simulate ribbon woven through the page.

6. Cut a double mat for photo. Adhere photo and mats together. Adhere matted photo to page. Mount rose sticker over mat.

7. Cut a triple rectangular mat for banner. Adhere mats together. Personalize banner, using brown pen. Mount heart sticker on banner. Mount banner above photo.

Specific Materials & Tools

Embossing tools
Permanent pen: brown
Scissors: decorative-edged
Stickers: heart, rose

39

Chapter Four
Frames

Photos have been resting inside frames for ages. This is still a simple, but effective way to highlight photos for all occasions. A traditional picture frame has an opening in the shape of an oval or rectangle and this is still a practical way to decorate a scrapbook page. Many other shapes, such as hearts, trees, and even bus windows, offer an alternative to traditional shapes.

The following techniques are used to create frames:

- Circles, ovals, rectangles, and square templates of many sizes are available in craft and department stores.

- Cut your own unique shape from lightweight cardstock.

- Use the Cutout Patterns on pages 100–120 to create a negative shape for a special frame that reinforces the theme of the photos. For example, two sweet-hearts can be placed inside heart-shaped frames, outdoor photos can be framed inside tree frames, and school photos set inside apple frames for an A+ presentation.

Aloha

Specific Materials & Tools

Cutout patterns: Frame, Hawaiian Lei, letters, Palm Tree #2, Rose, Tiny Flowers

Stickers: hearts

Instructions

1-5. Follow steps in General Project Steps on page 6.

6. Embellish cutouts as shown.

7. Crop around subjects' heads. Do not crop subjects completely away from photo.

8. Position photo behind frame. Adhere to page, using glue stick. Leave cropped area free.

9. Mount Hawaiian Lei on photo, slipping lei behind cropped area.

10. Cut strips from paper for border, using paper trimmer. Embellish page with border strips and heart stickers.

11. Mount letters, Palm Tree, Rose, and Tiny Flowers on page.

"Fun in the sun."

Heart Quilt

Specific Materials & Tools

Cutout pattern: Heart #1B
Stickers: hearts

Instructions

1-3. Follow steps 1, 3, and 5 in General Project Steps on page 6.

4. Cut four 4" squares, four 4¼" squares, nine 1" squares, and six 10" x ½" strips from papers, using paper trimmer.

5. Trace Heart #1B in center of each 4" paper. Cut out hearts to make frames.

6. Crop photos to fit frames. Center and adhere photos behind frame.

7. Center and mount frames on 4¼" papers. Mount matted frames on page, leaving ½" between frames.

8. Mount strips between and around outside edges of frames. Mount 1" paper squares on corners of each frame. Mount heart sticker on center of each 1" square.

Bus Buddies

The back of this school bus has a window opening that is a perfect frame for school photos.
An apple license plate reinforces the school theme.

Specific Materials & Tools

Cutout patterns:	Apple, School Bus Back
Permanent Pen:	black, silver
Stickers:	hearts, letters

"Don't forget an apple for the teacher."

Instructions

1-5. Follow steps in General Project Steps on page 6.

6. Cut a rectangular banner, using paper trimmer.

7. Embellish cutouts and banner as shown. Draw treads on tires, using silver pen.

8. Crop photos. Adhere photos to inside of School Bus Back, using glue stick.

9. Mount bus on page. Mount banner above bus.

10. Draw a line border around inside edges of page, using black pen.

43

Hunting for Chestnuts

HUNTING FOR CHESTNUTS

Instructions

Note: A scenery photo with coordinating background was enlarged on a color photocopier and used for this project.

1-5. Follow steps in General Project Steps on page 6.

6. Embellish cutouts as shown.

7. Cut an 8½" square from paper for frame, using paper trimmer. Trace desired number of Christmas Tree cutouts on frame and cut out. **Note:** The negative space of the Christmas Tree is used to frame the photos. The positive cutout is saved for other projects.

8. Crop photos as needed and adhere behind frame openings, using glue stick.

9. Cut a mat for frame, using paper trimmer. Adhere frame to mat and mat to page.

10. Cut four 8¼" x ¼" strips and Christmas Tree from background color copy. Punch maple leaves from color copy.

11. Adhere strips to frame for border. Trim ends of strips at angle so strips fit together evenly. Mount cutouts on page, using foam dots.

12. Personalize page with letter stickers.

13. Adhere maple leaves to page as desired.

Specific Materials & Tools

Craft punch: maple leaf
Cutout patterns: Christmas Tree, Pinecone
Foam dots
Stickers: letters

"Autumn leaves fell down as quickly as you grew up."

Love

A simple way to frame a photo is with repeated contrasting color mats placed behind or around the photo, with each mat increasing in size. Some mats can be plain and some patterned, based on personal preference. Mats can be made from rectangles, squares, or strips cut to size.

Specific Materials
& Tools

Cutout pattern: "Love"
Stickers: border, hearts

"Eskimo and Butterfly
kisses for you!"

Instructions

1-5. Follow steps in General Project Steps on page 6.

6. Cut patterned paper to fit entire scrapbook page, using paper trimmer. Adhere paper to page, using glue stick, or mount with mounting adhesive sheets.

7. Mount photo on colored mat.

8. Cut mats on various colored paper, each progressively larger. Stack mats, with photo in center.

9. Cut small squares from paper and adhere to corners of second mat. Mount heart stickers on centers of squares.

10. Mount mats with photo on page.

11. Mount "Love" cutout along center top of frame.

12. Embellish page with border and heart stickers.

Chapter Five
Borders

A border serves to visually complete a scrapbook page. Placing a border on a page creates a finished look comparable to what a mat does for a photo or frame for a picture.

The following techniques are used to create borders:

- **Rulers** with either straight or decorative edges and colored pens are a fast, simple border technique.

- **Stickers** lined up in a row or decorative borders stickers make wonderful border solutions.

- **Multiple mats** around pictures may be used to create the feeling of a border.

PRO
NIG

DAVE & LISA

Prom Night

Specific Materials & Tools

Cutout patterns: Banner, Plain Photo Corners
Stickers: hearts, letters, numbers, roses, checkered border

Instructions

1-5. Follow steps in General Project Steps on page 6.

6. Cut a double rectangular mat for bottom banner and a single mat for photo, using paper trimmer.

7. Adhere photo to single mat, using glue stick. Adhere photo corner cutouts to mat. Adhere mat to page.

8. Mount banners above and below photo. Personalize banners with letter, number, and rose stickers.

9. Embellish page with stripe border and heart stickers.

BASS LAKE

YOSEMITE

Bass Lake

A black pen and ruler, decorative-edged scissors, and pinecones combine for this border effect.

Specific Materials & Tools

Cutout patterns: Country Road Sign, Fish Hook, Pinecone, Row Boat
Photo corners: black
Permanent pen: black
Scissors: decorative-edged

Instructions

1-5. Follow steps in General Project Steps on page 6.

6. Embellish cutouts as shown. Personalize road sign, using black pen.

7. Cut a double mat for photo. Adhere photo to top mat, using glue stick. Draw a line border around outside edges of photo, using black pen. Mount photo corners to corners of mat. Mount top mat on bottom mat. Mount double mat on page.

8. Draw a line border around outside edges of largest mat, using black pen.

9. Cut a strip from paper for water to fit across bottom of page. Trim top edge, using decorative-edged scissors. Mount water on page.

10. Mount cutouts on page.

11. Draw splash marks around oar, using black pen.

"May all roads lead to great memories."

Deck the Halls

Specific Materials & Tools

Cutout patterns: Decorative Photo Corners
Stickers: hearts, holly, letters, bow

Instructions

1-5. Follow steps in General Project Steps on page 6.

6. Cut a double mat for photo and a double rectangular mat for banner, using paper trimmer. Mount mats together as shown.

7. Embellish banner with holly and letter stickers.

8. Adhere photo to top mat, using glue stick. Place photo corners on matted photo. Mount bow sticker on photo corner cutout.

9. Mount photo corners with mat on page. Mount banner above matted photo.

10. Embellish page with heart stickers.

DECK THE HALLS

A Star is Born

Here is a perfect example of how to highlight one really special photo on a scrapbook page.

Instructions

1-5. Follow steps in General Project Steps on page 6.

6. Cut a mat for photo, using paper trimmer. Adhere photo to mat, using glue stick. Mount mat to page.

7. Draw a line border around outside edges of mat, using black pen. Mount polka-dot border and heart stickers around line border.

8. Crop photos to fit inside film strip cutout. Adhere photos to film strip. Mount film strip on page.

9. Cut mats for stripe border stickers. Mount stickers on mats. Mount mats and heart stickers on page.

10. Personalize page with letter and number stickers.

Specific Materials & Tools

Cutout pattern: Filmstrip #2
Permanent pen: black
Stickers: hearts, letters, numbers, polka-dot border, stripe border

Hosts of "The View"

These scrapbook pages were created in conjunction with an appearance by Sandi Genovese on The View. This double-page spread illustrates two types of borders.

Specific Materials & Tools

Cutout patterns: Director Chair, Light Beam, Primitive Star, Spot Light

Foam dots
Permanent pen: gold
Stickers: stars, stripe border,

Instructions

1-5. Follow steps in General Project Steps on page 6.

6. Embellish cutouts as shown. Personalize Director Chairs, using gold pen.

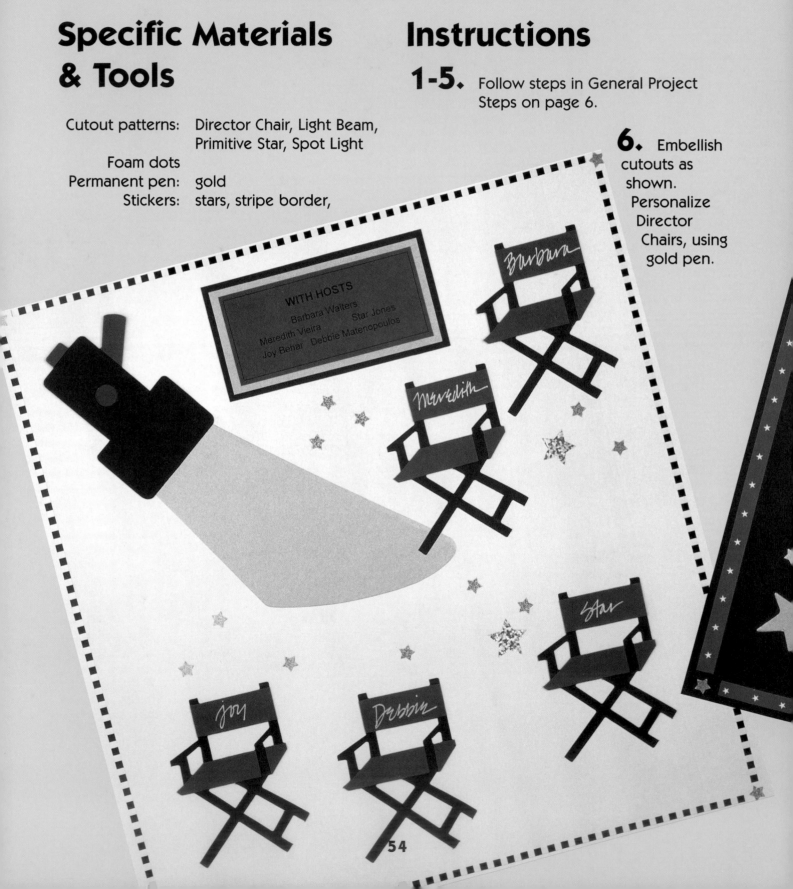

WITH HOSTS

Barbara Walters
Meredith Vieira   Star Jones
Joy Behar   Debbie Matenopoulos

54

7. Cut a triple mat for banner, using paper trimmer. Personalize top mat, using computer or typewriter. Mount mats together. Mount banner on page.

8. Mount Director Chairs, Light Beam, stripe border and star stickers on page.

9. Crop photos. Adhere photos to page, using glue stick.

10. Adhere "seated" photo to Director Chair. Mount Director Chair on page.

11. Cut strips from paper for border. Mount borders on page.

12. Mount Primitive Star on page, using foam dot.

13. Embellish page with star cutouts and stickers.

Photos are provided courtesy of ABC News, The View.

Little Dippers

Specific Materials & Tools

Craft punch:	duck
Cutout patterns:	Bathtub, Middle Wave, Toy Duck, Water Splash, Whale
Foam dots	
Permanent Pen:	blue, orange
Stickers:	flowers, letters

Instructions

1-5. Follow steps in General Project Steps on page 6.

6. Embellish cutouts as shown.

7. Cut mats for photos, using paper trimmer. Adhere photos to mats, using glue stick. Mount mats on pages.

8. Cut two triple rectangular mats for banners. Punch ducks in top mats, using craft punch. Set punch outs aside for later use. Mount mats together. Mount banners on pages.

9. Crop photos.

10. Adhere cropped photo in bathtub. Mount bathtub on page.

11. Mat cropped photo. Mount flower sticker on photo. Mount photo on page, using foam dots.

12. Mount offset wave cutouts together. Mount waves on pages, using foam dots.

13. Color beaks and eyes on duck punch outs, using orange and blue pens. Adhere ducks to pages.

14. Mat splash cutouts. Mount splashes on page, using foam dots.

15. Embellish page with remaining cutouts and letter stickers.

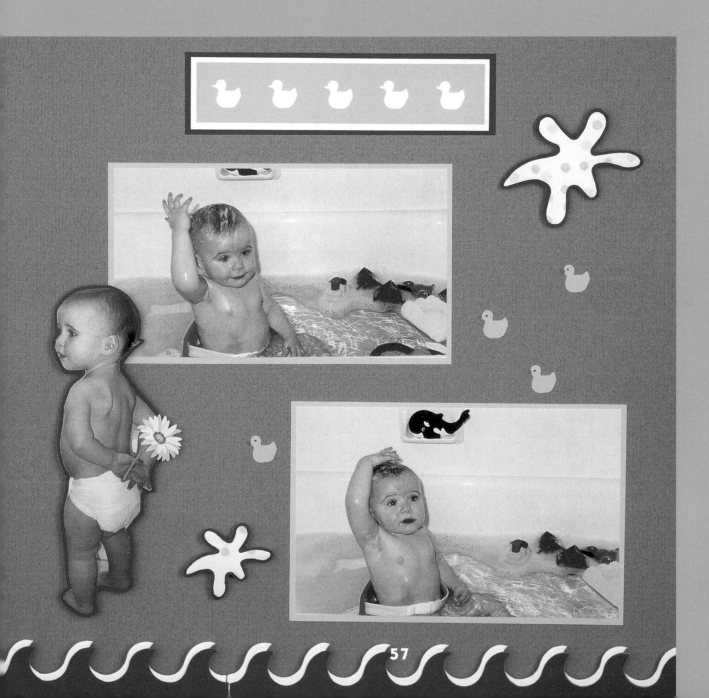

Chapter Six
Interactive

How can you keep scrapbook pages from becoming boring? Animate them! Create interactive pages that draw viewers in, letting them lift, pull, and open various elements. These pages are great fun and make even the most ordinary photos jump right off the page. Assembling animated scrapbook pages is simple and the results are sensational!

Animation involves various types of folds. The folded pop-up mechanism generally sits within the cover of a pop-up card. The back of the cover is mounted directly onto a scrapbook page, while the front cover – decorated with photos, cutouts, stickers, or rubber stamps – effectively hides the photo inside until the viewer lifts, pulls, or opens the card. The animated portion springs to life, catching the unsuspecting viewer by surprise.

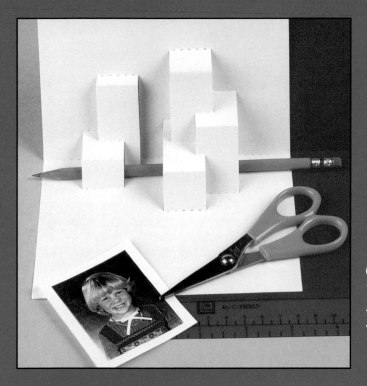

The following steps apply to pop-up card assembly:

1. Cut pop-up card patterns to desired dimensions, using one of several Cutout Patterns on pages 100–120. Dotted lines indicate a fold line. Solid lines indicate a cut line. Heavier-weight papers will need to be scored lightly before folding along dotted lines, using a craft knife. Fold card in half.

2. Fold each tab as shown.

3. Open card. Push pop-up tab away from fold, creasing fold of pop-up tab in the opposite direction. Close card, folding pop-up tab inside.

4. Cut separate cover for card ½" larger than pop-up card. Fold cover in half. Cover should completely hide pictures inside. Center and adhere cover to pop-up card, using glue stick.

5. Adhere photo(s) to pop-up tabs, using glue stick.

6. Mount pop-up card to page. Embellish card with photo, cutout, and stickers.

The following steps apply to "dangle" pop-up card assembly:

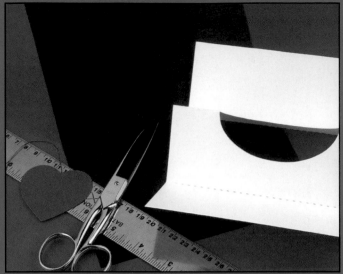

1. Cut Accordionwith Cutout, using Cutout Pattern on page 102. Dotted lines indicate a fold line. Solid lines indicate a cut line. Cut card to desired dimensions. Cut separate cover for card ½" larger than pop-up card. Fold card in half.

2. Place a small piece of thread between heart cutouts. Mount heart cutouts together. Personalize heart, using letter and number stickers.

3. Attach heart to under-side of pop-up, using tape, allowing heart to dangle in center of oval pop-up tab. Adhere Accordion Card to cover, using glue stick. Only top and bottom panel should be adhered to scrapbook page. Do not adhere two middle panels to card cover.

4. Adhere photos to inside of card. Embellish card as desired.

5. Fold card. Cut a heart frame for top of card. Adhere photo behind frame. Adhere frame to top of card.

The following steps apply to envelope or memorabilia pocket assembly:

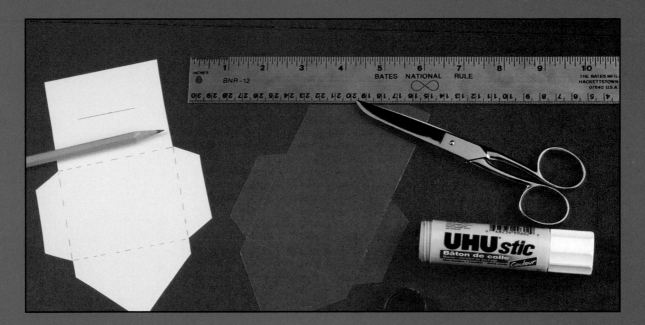

1. Cut envelope to desired dimensions from paper or clear page protector, using Gift Card with Insert (Gift Card only) Cutout Pattern on page 109, or an unfolded envelope. Dotted lines indicate a fold line. Solid lines indicate a cut line. Heavier-weight papers will need to be scored lightly before folding along dotted lines, using a craft knife.

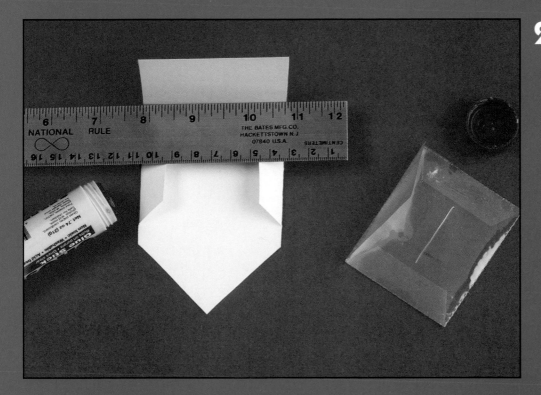

2. Fold side flaps toward center of envelope. Mount to inside edges of bottom flap with double-sided tape. Fold bottom flap up and adhere to side of flaps. Contrasting card insert can be slipped inside memorabilia pocket to visually separate pocket from page. Note: Envelope flap slides into slit for temporary closure.

The following steps apply to slider card assembly:

1. Cut Slider Card Cover to desired dimensions from heavyweight cardstock, using Cutout Patterns on page 118. Dotted lines indicate a fold line. Solid lines indicate a cut line. Heavier-weight papers will need to be scored lightly before folding along dotted lines, using a craft knife.

2. Cut Slider Card from lightweight cardstock, using Cutout Patterns on page 118. Solid lines indicate a cut line.
   Note: Slider Card Cover should always be enlarged the same percentage as Slider Card.

3. Cut mat for photo to sit on Slider Card large enough to hide photo on inside of Slider Card Cover.

4. Slide flap of Slider Card into slit of Slider Card Cover.

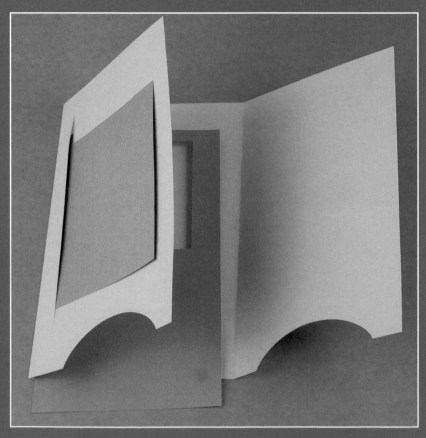

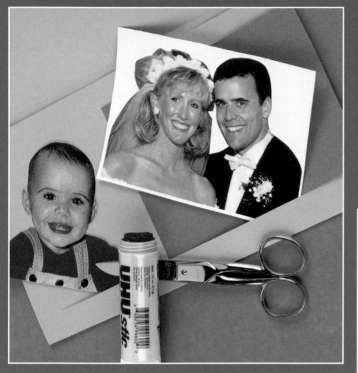

5. Mount matted Slider Card photo on Slider Card, using glue stick. Align bottom left corner of mat with bottom left corner of Slider Card flap.

6. Pull slider to right. Mount inside Slider Card Cover photo above slit. Push Slider Card left to cover this photo.
Note: You should be able to see both photos when slider is pulled to right. Only one photo can be seen when slider is pushed to left.

7. Fold Slider Card Cover. Cut mat for photo on outside of Slider Card Cover. Mount photo on mat. Mount matted photo on outside of Slider Card Cover.

Grin & Bare It

The photo on the cover of this pop-up card shows the day the child's braces were put on, surrounding photos were taken during the time braces were on, and photo inside chronicles the day braces were removed.

Specific Materials & Tools

Cutout patterns: Gift Card with Insert, letters, Lips, Pop-up Card #1B, Toothbrush & Tooth, Toothpaste
Page protector: clear
Permanent Pen: black, silver
Stickers: letters, numbers

Instructions

1-5. Follow steps in General Project Steps on page 6.

6. Embellish cutouts as shown. Draw teeth and braces on lips, using black and silver pens.

7. Follow steps 1–5 in pop-up card assembly on page 59. Cut a cover for card, using paper trimmer. Adhere card to cover, using glue stick. Do not adhere pop-up tab to cover.

8. Crop photos. Mat one photo and adhere to pop-up tab. Personalize card with letter and number stickers.

9. Make memorabilia envelope from clear page protector, following envelope or memorabilia pocket assembly on page 61. Cut card insert from desired paper. Tuck tooth cutout inside envelope or enclose real tooth.

10. Cut paper to fit page. Adhere paper to page.

11. Mount pop-up card and memorabilia pocket to page.

12. Embellish page with photos and cutouts.

School Days

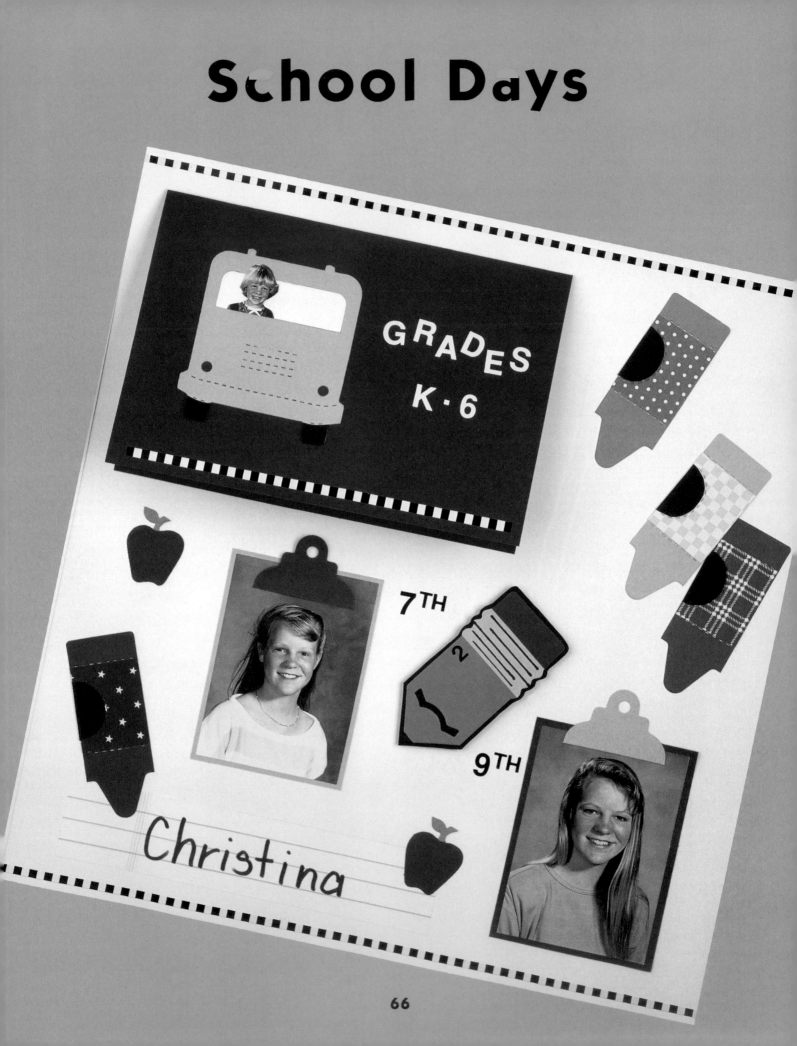

GRADES
K·6

7TH

9TH

Christina

Instructions

1-5. Follow steps in General Project Steps on page 6.

6. Embellish cutouts as shown. Color tip of pencil, using black pen.

7. Follow steps 1–5 in pop-up card assembly on page 59. Cut a cover for card, using paper trimmer. Adhere cover to card, using glue stick. Do not adhere pop-up tabs to cover.

8. Crop photos. Mount pop-up on page, using School Bus Back as frame.

9. Adhere cropped photos to pop-up tabs and to card. Cut a double rectangular mat for banner inside card. Adhere mats together. Personalize banner, using silver pen. Embellish inside of card with cutouts and stickers.

10. Use Clipboard cutouts as mats for photos. Adhere photos to clipboards. Mount clipboards on page. Mount one pencil on page, using foam dot.

Specific Materials & Tools

Cutout patterns: Clipboard, Crayon, Pencil, Multiple Pop-up Card, School Bus Back, Tiny Apples

Foam dot

Permanent Pen: black, red, silver

Stickers: stripe border, letters, numbers

11. Cut a rectangular mat from notebook paper for banner. Personalize banner, using red pen. Mount banner on page.

12. Embellish page with remaining cutouts and stickers.

"B" is for Burt

These scrapbook pages were created in conjunction with an appearance by Sandi Genovese on The View.

Specific Materials & Tools

Cutout patterns: Clipboard, Filmstrip #1, letters, Multiple Pop-up Card, Primitive Stars

Permanent Pen: black, silver

Stickers: hearts, letters, checkered border

Instructions

1-5. Follow steps in General Project Steps on page 6.

6. Embellish cutouts as shown.

7. Follow steps 1–5 in pop-up card assembly on page 59. Cut a cover

BURT REYNOLDS

for card, using paper trimmer. Adhere card to cover, using glue stick. Do not adhere pop-up tabs to cover.

8. Crop photos. Adhere photos to tabs. Mount star on inside of card.

9. Cut a double mat for card. Mount mats together. Adhere card to mats. Mount matted card on page.

10. Draw line borders around outside edges of photo and mat, using silver pen and ruler.

11. Draw a border around outside edges of mat, using black pen and ruler.

12. Adhere photos to back side of Filmstrip #1. Mount filmstrip on page.

13. Cut a mat for photo. Adhere photo to mat. Mount mat on page. Draw a line border around outside edges of mat, using black pen and ruler.

14. Embellish pages with cut-outs and stickers.

Photos are provided courtesy of ABC News, The View.

Christmas

Colored mats are used on this angel theme page to draw the eye to the center of the page. Open the three-dimensional card and the photo literally pops off the page.

Specific Materials & Tools

Cutout patterns: Angel, 3-D card
Permanent Pen: silver
Stickers: checkered border, hearts, holly, letters, roses, stars

"What a tree-mendous Christmas!"

Instructions

1-5. Follow steps in General Project Steps on page 6.

6. Embellish Angel cutout as shown.

7. Fold card as indicated. Dotted lines indicate a fold line. Solid lines indicate a cut line. Cut a cover for card, using paper trimmer. Adhere card to cover, using glue stick. Do not adhere pop-up tab to cover.

8. Crop photo to fit pop-up tab. Cut photo in center along fold line of tab to prevent tearing. Adhere photo to tab.

9. Embellish inside of card with holly, letter, and checkered border stickers.

10. Mount Angel on cover of card.

11. Cut mat for page. Adhere mat to page. Adhere card to mat.

12. Draw a line border around outside edges of mat, using silver pen.

13. Embellish page with star and checkered border stickers.

71

New Mexico

These scrapbook pages were created in conjunction with an appearance by Sandi Genovese on Good Morning America.

These two scrapbook pages have a unique pop-up feature. The act of opening the pages allows the element to lift off the page. This technique will only work with an album that has a seam between the pages. It will not work with a three-ring binder album. A pattern or die-cut is used to cut out the pop-up feature. The pattern can be enlarged to fit the photo.

Specific Materials & Tools

Cutout patterns: Double Pop-up, Mission, Pitcher, Square, Triangle

Stickers: assorted borders

Instructions

1-5. Follow steps in General Project Steps on page 6.

6. Embellish cutouts as shown.

7. Cut paper to fit pages, using paper trimmer. Adhere paper to pages, using glue stick or double-sided tape.

8. Cut double mats for photos. Mount mats together. Adhere photos to mats. Mount matted photos on pages.

9. Fold card as indicated. Crop photo to fit pop-up. Adhere photo to pop-up. Adhere pop-up to pages as shown, using scrapbook glue.

10. Mount cutouts to page as shown.

Photos are provided courtesy of ABC News – Good Morning America.

Kissing Cousins

Specific Materials & Tools

Cutout patterns: Accordion with Cutout, Heart #2, Ladder, Lips

Foam dot Stickers: hearts, letters, numbers

1984

1980

1992

KISSING COUSINS

1987

Instructions

1-5. Follow steps in General Project Steps on page 6.

6. Embellish cutouts as shown.

7. Follow steps in pop-up card assembly on page 60. Cut cover for card, using paper trimmer. Fold cover in half. Adhere card to inside of cover, using glue stick. Do not adhere pop-up tab to cover. Adhere card to page.

8. Crop photos. Mat one cropped photo.

9. Cut a mat for uncropped photo. Adhere photo to mat. Mount mat on page.

10. Embellish page with remaining cropped photos, cutouts, and stickers. Mount matted cropped photo, using foam dot.

We Really Grew Some

WE REALLY GREW SOME

PULL

LIFT FIRST

Specific Materials & Tools

Cutout patterns: numbers, Middle Flowers,
                  Slider Card, Slider Card
                  Cover
Stickers: flowers, hearts, letters

Instructions

1-5. Follow steps in General Project Steps on page 6.

6. Embellish cutouts as shown.

7. Follow steps in slider card assembly on pages 62–63.

8. Personalize card with stickers and cutouts.

9. Cut mat for card. Adhere card to mat.

10. Embellish page with cutouts and stickers. Mount matted card on page.

77

"Z" Is for Baez

These scrapbook pages were created in conjunction with an appearance by Sandi Genovese on The View. This double-page spread uses the accordion-fold card for animation. The accordion pleats are used as furrows to display photos. The photos will be enhanced even more, if the subjects are cropped before they are attached. Subjects in the photos on the accordion card are cropped from the same photos shown uncropped on the page.

Specific Materials & Tools

Cutout patterns:	Accordion Card, Guitar, letters, Musical Notes MX, Primitive Stars
Foam dots	
Permanent Pen:	gold
Stickers:	letters, polka-dot border, stars, stripe border
Thread:	black

JOAN BAEZ

Instructions

1-5. Follow steps in General Project Steps on page 6. Do not adhere mounting adhesive sheets to Accordion Card Cutout Pattern.

6. Embellish cutouts as shown. Cut guitar strings from black thread and adhere to back of guitar, using tape.

7. Fold Accordion Card, creating a front and back cover with pleats inside. Dotted lines indicate a fold line. Cut cover for card, using paper trimmer. Fold cover in half. Adhere front and back of card to inside of cover, using glue stick. Do not adhere accordion folds to cover.

8. Crop photos. Adhere photos to accordion pleats, using glue stick.

9. Embellish top of card with cutouts and stickers. Mount card to page.

10. Cut mats for photos. Adhere photos to mats. Mount mats on pages. Mount cropped photo on page, using foam dots.

11. Embellish page with cutouts and stickers. Mount some cutouts, using foam dots.

Photos are provided courtesy of ABC News, The View

Happy Birthday

Specific Materials & Tools

Cutout patterns: Balloons, Tiny Balloons, "Birthday", Birthday Cake with Candle (candle only), Gift with Ribbon, "Happy", Party Noisemaker #2, Nose, Multiple Pop-up, Sunglasses

Foam dot
Imitation fur
Permanent Pen: silver
Stickers: stars

Instructions

1-5. Follow steps in General Project Steps on pages 6.

6. Embellish cutouts as shown. Embellish party noisemaker, using foam dot.

7. Follow steps 1–5 in pop-up card assembly on page 59. Cut cover for card, using paper trimmer. Fold cover in half. Adhere card to inside of cover, using glue stick. Do not adhere pop-up tabs to cover.

8. Crop photos. Adhere cropped photos to tabs. Embellish inside of card, adhering several balloons to one tab.

9. Cut mats for photos. Adhere photos to mats. Mount matted photos on pages.

10. Mount pop-up card on page. Draw a line border around outside edges of mat, using silver pen. Embellish top of card.

11. Cut border strips from paper. Mount border strips around inside edges of pages.

12. Embellish pages with remaining cropped photo, cutouts, and stickers.

"A special day to celebrate!"

Vail

Specific Materials & Tools

Craft punches: large, small snowflake
Cutout patterns: Christmas Tree #2, Mitten, Mountain Range Border, Pop-up #1B, Skier
Foam dots
Stickers: border, hearts, letters

Instructions

1-5. Follow steps in General Project Steps on pages 6.

6. Embellish cutouts as shown.

7. Follow steps 1–5 in pop-up card assembly on page 59. Cut cover for card, using paper trimmer. Fold cover in half. Adhere card to inside of cover, using glue stick. Do not adhere pop-up tab to cover.

8. Crop photos. Adhere one cropped photo to tab.

9. Cut a curvy line to resemble string. Adhere string and Mitten to inside of card.

10. Cut a mat for top of card. Mount

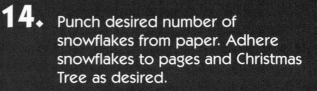

14. Punch desired number of snowflakes from paper. Adhere snowflakes to pages and Christmas Tree as desired.

15. Embellish pages with remaining cutouts and stickers. Personalize pages with letter stickers.

VAIL

Christmas Trees on mat, mounting one using foam dots. Adhere card to page.

11. Cut mats for photos. Adhere photos to mats. Mount mats on pages.

12. Mount border stickers around inside edges of pages.

13. Position cropped photos along Mountain Border, overlapping portions of photos on front of ranges. Mount Mountain Range Border and adhere photos to bottom of pages.

'98

Chapter Seven
Beyond Scrapbooking

Most of the tools and supplies used to create scrapbook pages can also be used for a number of other craft projects. This chapter is designed to illustrate the wide variety of items that can be made using the various supplies you already have. The list of projects is unending and the personal satisfaction that comes from "individualizing" your projects is boundless.

- Personalized greeting cards for Christmas and other holidays

- Novelty plant sticks

- Party invitations

- Holiday decorations

- Any number of unique gifts for the special people in your life

Hanging Around

This spiral bear mobile is fun and simple to make. Cut out the Spiral Bonus Cutout Pattern in Bonus Cutout Patterns on pages 121–126 from heavyweight cardstock as the base for your favorite thematic shapes. Embellish the cutouts of your choice. Follow step 3 in "dangle" pop-up card assembly on page 60 for attaching cutouts to spiral.

84

Way To Go

Accordion cards are perfect for showing enthusiasm. From a job well done, to hugs and kisses, this card is full of possibilities.

Follow steps 7–8 in Z is for Baez on page 79 for card assembly. Embellish cutouts as desired.

CLAP

APPLAUSE

TREEMENDOUS

You're Invited

Colorful cardstock cutouts allow you to create wonderful invitations in your own unique style. Die-cuts, stickers, and colored pens add to the possibilities!

Follow steps in memorabilia pocket instructions on page 61, creating four envelope flaps instead of one. Embellish card as desired. Seal envelope with a sticker. Once envelope is sealed it can be addressed on the flip side and mailed.

LUNCH & LEMONADE

You're Invited

NAME _____
PLACE _____
DATE _____
TIME _____
PHONE _____

Celebrate

I Hope your Holidays are

Get Well Soon

Nothing makes a person feel better than knowing someone cares. A handmade get well card is extra special.

Follow steps in memorabilia pocket instructions on page 61. Fill with shapes from a craft punch for a "fun filled" announcement or invitation.

OUCH

you're A star

SORRY

From the Heart

Love comes in many forms, whether it be a heartfelt thank-you or red-hot peppers.

Make a card or cover using heavyweight cardstock. Embellish cutouts with small stickers. Personalize, using metallic pens. Make a book by binding your collection with a plastic comb binder that is available at most copy centers.

Thank You

RECIPES

HOT HOT HOT

Celebrate

Plants are great gifts that grow with time, but can be hard to wrap. Novelty plant sticks are a perfect solution. All you need are cutouts or die-cuts and sticks.

Embellish and mat cutouts as desired. Mount on sticks with tape.

Thanks a Bunch

A simple thank-you can mean so much. Layering the word "Thanks" helps to convey a deep appreciation. Small heart stickers and a border drawn with a metallic pen complete these simple but meaningful cards. Envelopes cut from clear page protectors let the color shine through.

Follow steps in memorabilia pocket instructions on page 61. Cut card from heavyweight cardstock. Embellish as desired.

Alyson—

Thank you so much for everything. I wouldn't have managed without you.

Love, Sam

Especially For You

Tried and true, the heart is the traditional symbol of love. Layer it. Emboss it. Embellish it.

The "Thanks" card says both thank you and I love you. Follow faux embossing technique on page 35.

Untie the bow of the heart card to reveal a heart-felt message.

On Valentine's Day

A handmade card is just the beginning. Decorate your own wrapping paper or make a unique gift box for an added special touch. Color coordinate envelopes with matching paper.

Follow steps in pop-up card assembly instructions on page 60 and memorabilia pocket assembly instructions on page 61.

Embellish each project with cutouts, rubber stamps, stickers, die-cuts, and metallic pens for something tailor-made for your sweetheart.

Journal of Love

What would be a more precious keepsake
than a handmade journal of your life
together?

Follow faux embossing technique on page 35.
Embellish with stickers and a silk ribbon to tie
it all together.

Cards of Endearment

Over the years, handmade cards can be collected for scrapbooking.

Follow "dangling" pop-up card assembly on page 60, making a vertical instead of a horizontal card.

Herb Garden

Spice up your herb garden with these colorful plant sticks. Carry the theme over to a book of favorite herbal recipes.

Follow plant stick instructions on page 89.

Tie the recipe book with a coordinating ribbon or use plastic rings for quick and easy assembly.

Deck the Halls

When it's time to set up the holiday
decorations, there's nothing like a Christmas
carol to set the mood.

Follow steps 7–8 in Z for Baez on page 79.
Add cutouts, a star sticker for the tree, and a
ribbon to tie it all together.

Merry Christmas

Christmastime is the perfect opportunity to let your imagination go wild! These interactive cards are fun to make, give, and receive.

The ornament card is a great example. Follow "dangle" pop-up card assembly on page 60, making a vertical instead of a horizontal card.

Wish your friends a "Merry Christmoose." The moose card is a charming three-dimensional work of art. It does not open; but when moved from side to side, it gives the appearance of a moose migration!

The moose card is made from two accordion cards (one with a window) adhered back to back. Moose die-cuts were mounted to bases cut to the width of the card and mounted between accordion folds.

...NOT A CREATURE WAS STIRRING, NOT EVEN A MOOSE.

98

This variation of the traditional pop-up card, when tied together, is a unique Christmas card, forming a pyramid.

Cut and assemble four Pyramid Card cutouts in Bonus Cutout Patterns on pages 121–126. Follow pop-up card assembly on page 59 as a basic guide, folding card as indicated. Mount cards back to back with double-sided tape. Embellish with cutouts, a ribbon, and stickers.

Cutout Patterns

The following cutout patterns are replicas of Ellison® dies. A corresponding die list is included on page 127. Solid lines indicate a cut line. Dotted lines may either indicate detail or a fold line. Do not cut patterns from book. Enlarge or reduce cutout patterns to desired dimensions with a copy machine.

0123456
789

ABCDEFG
HIJKLMNO
PQRSTUV
WXYZ?'(!)

0123456789

ABCDEFGHI

JKLMNOPQ

RSTYVWXYZ

abcdefghi

jklmnopqrs

tuvwxyz?'(!)

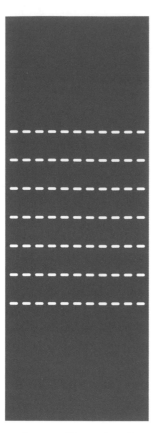

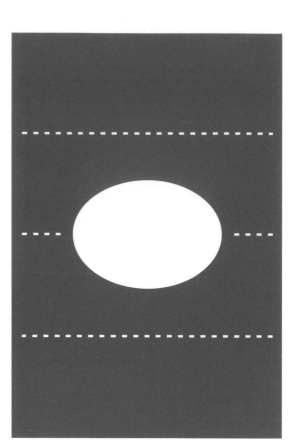

Accordion Card

Accordion with Cutout

Apple

Angel #1

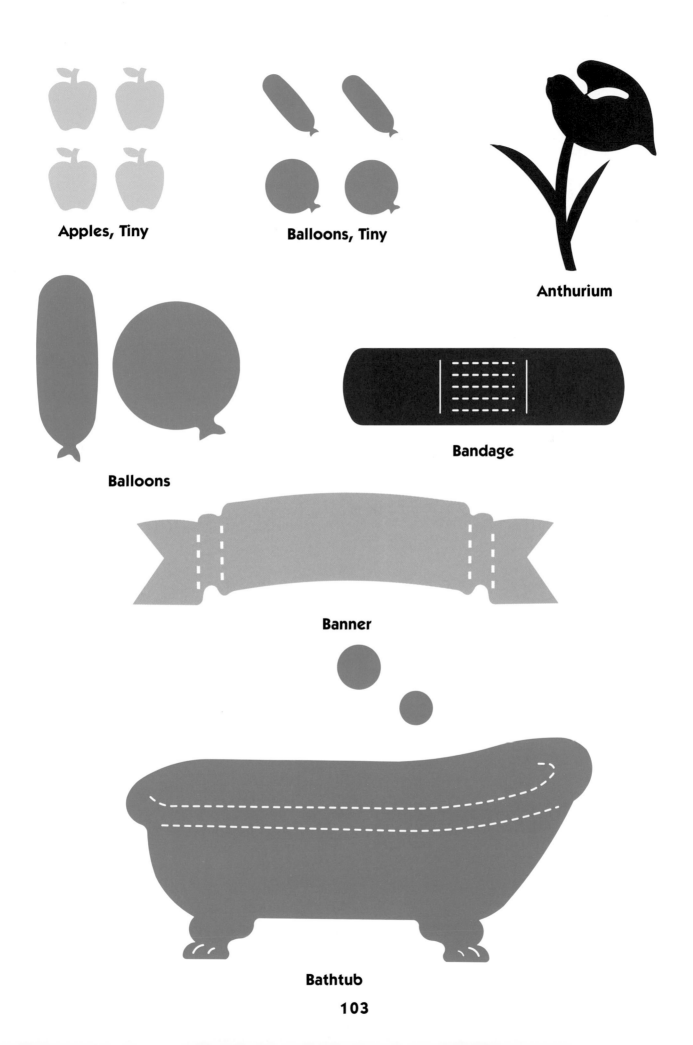

Apples, Tiny

Balloons, Tiny

Anthurium

Balloons

Bandage

Banner

Bathtub

Beach Ball

Bird #4

Bird #2A

Bird of Paradise

Bluebonnet

Bookmark, Heart

"Birthday"

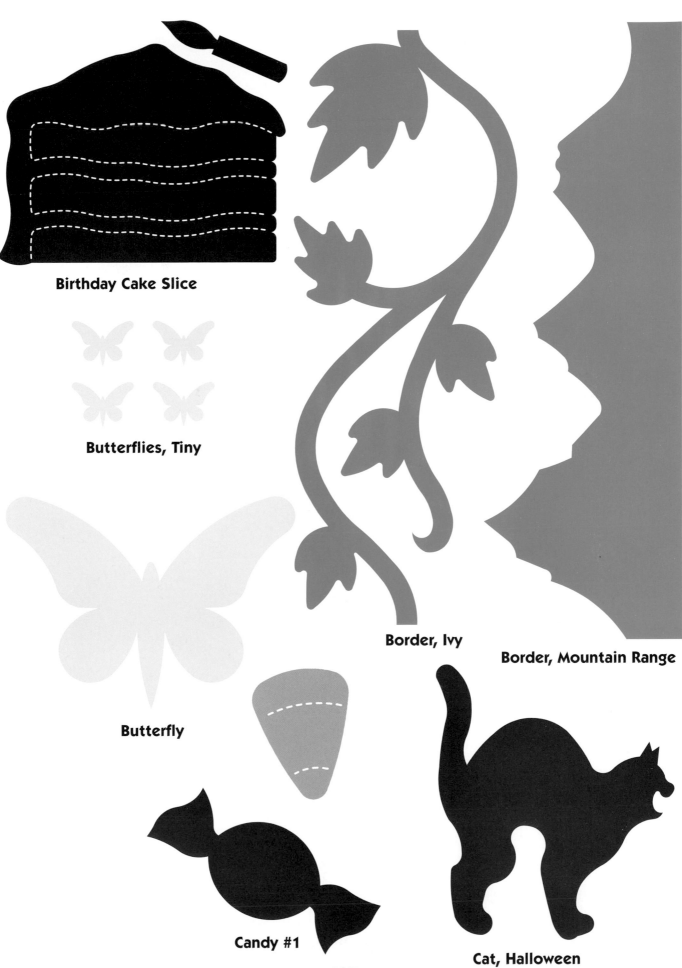

Birthday Cake Slice

Butterflies, Tiny

Butterfly

Border, Ivy

Border, Mountain Range

Candy #1

Cat, Halloween

105

3-D Card, Plain

Christmas Tree #2

Clipboard

Crayon

Daisy

"Congrats"

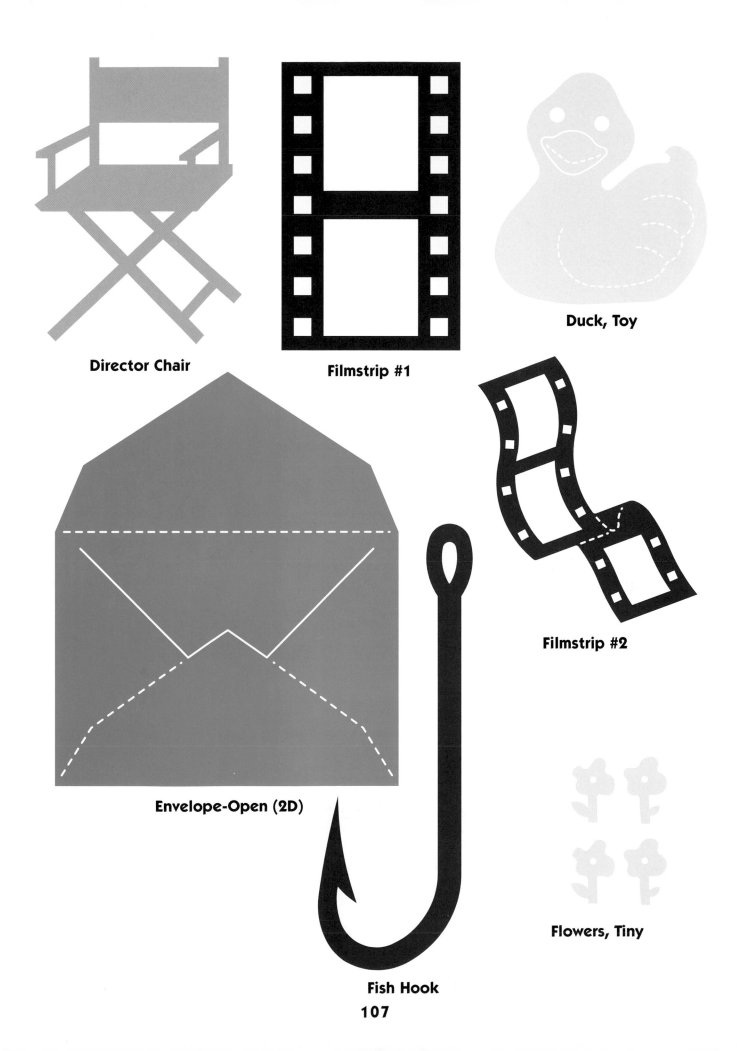

Director Chair

Filmstrip #1

Duck, Toy

Filmstrip #2

Envelope-Open (2D)

Fish Hook

Flowers, Tiny

Frame

Front/Umbrella (Diorama)

Ghost #2

Gift Card with Insert

Gift with Ribbon

Guitar

Hair Dryer

"Happy"

109

Hawaiian Lei

Heart, Primitive

Heart #1A

Heart #1B

Heart #2

Hearts, Tiny

Holly

Ladder

Iris

111

Light, Spot

Leaves, Tiny

Light Beam

Lips

"Love"

Middle/Flowers (Diorama)

Middle/Waves (Diorama)

112

Mission

Mitten

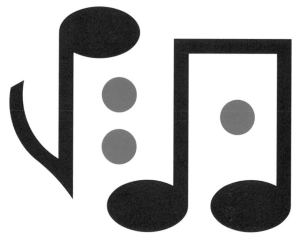

Musical Notes MX

Palm Tree #2

Nose

Party Noisemaker #2

Pencil

Pine Cone

Pitcher

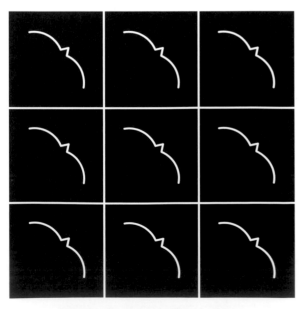

Photo Corners, Decorative

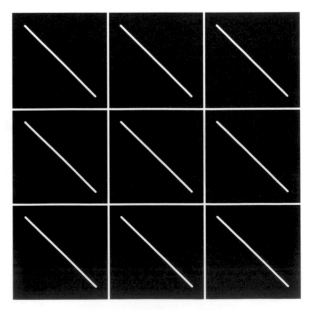

Photo Corners, Plain

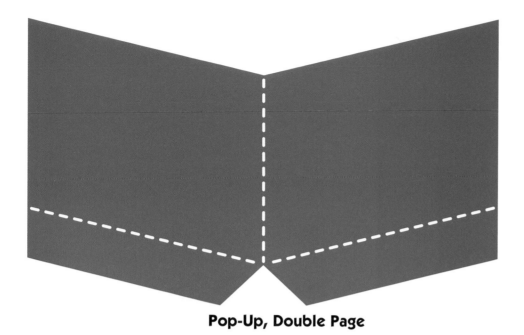

Pop-Up, Double Page

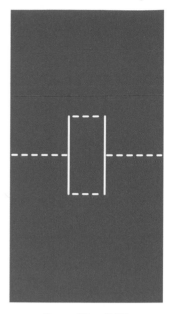

Pop-Up #1B

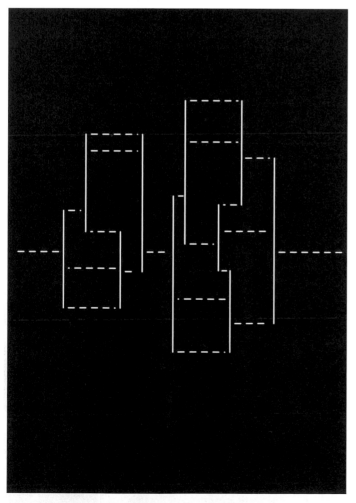

Pop-Up, Multiple

Pumpkin #1A

Pumpkin #1B

Row Boat

Road Sign, Country

Rose

Scissors

School Bus Back

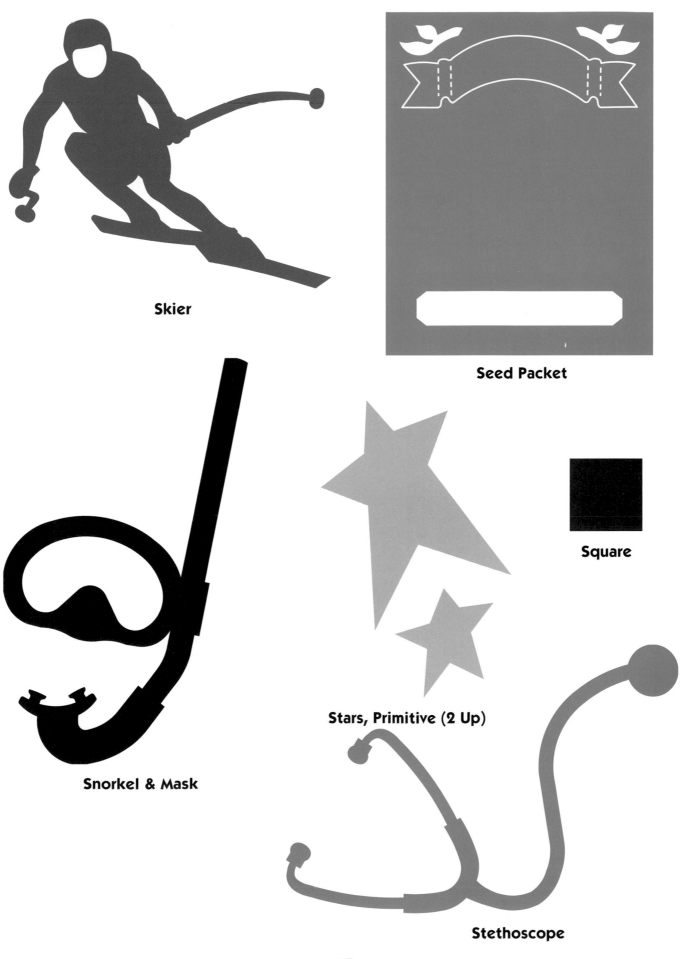

Skier

Seed Packet

Square

Stars, Primitive (2 Up)

Snorkel & Mask

Stethoscope

117

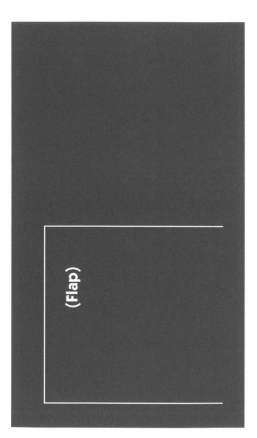

Slider Card

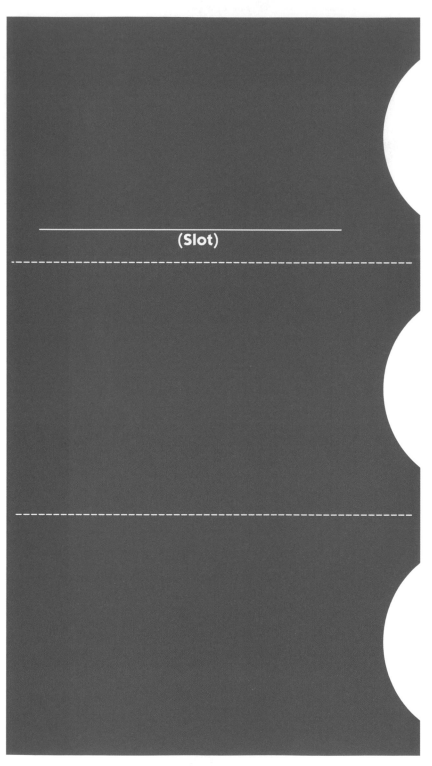

(Slot)

(Flap)

Slider Card Cover

Sunglasses

Sunflower

"Thanks"

Toothbrush & Tooth

Toothpaste

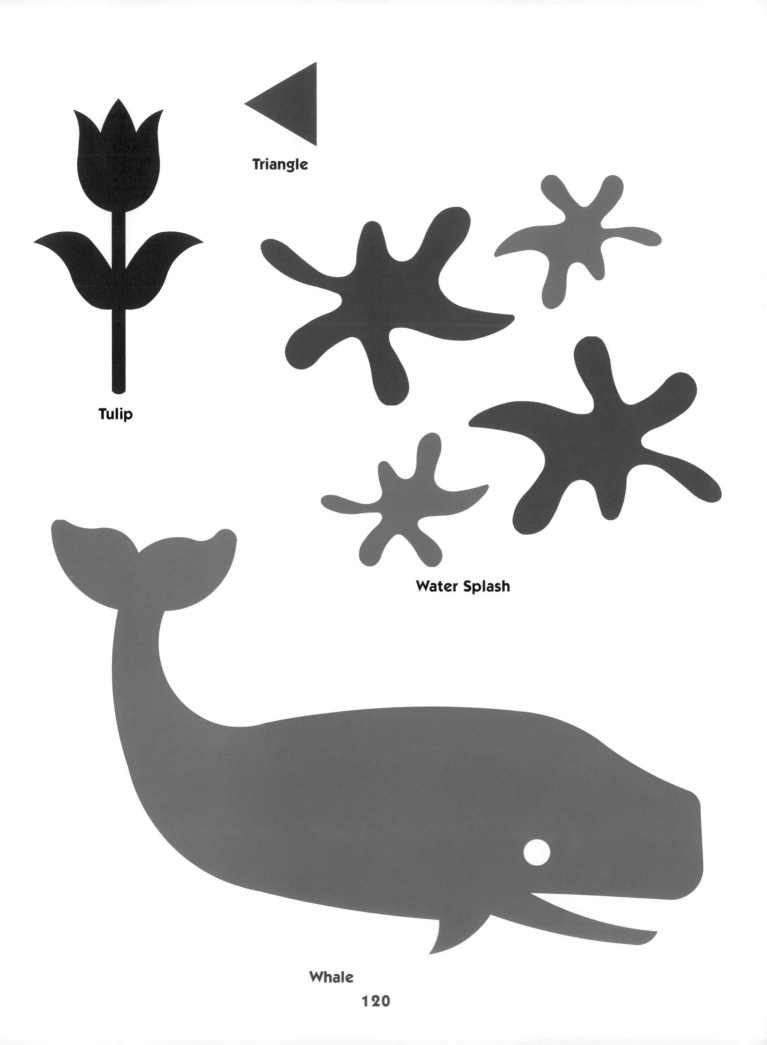

Triangle

Tulip

Water Splash

Whale

Bonus Cutout Patterns

Acorn

Airplane #2

Baby Booties

Bat

Bear

Beach Chair #2

Border, Bats

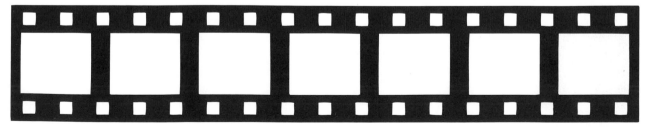

Border, Fence

Border, Filmstrip

Border, Grass

Border, Southwest

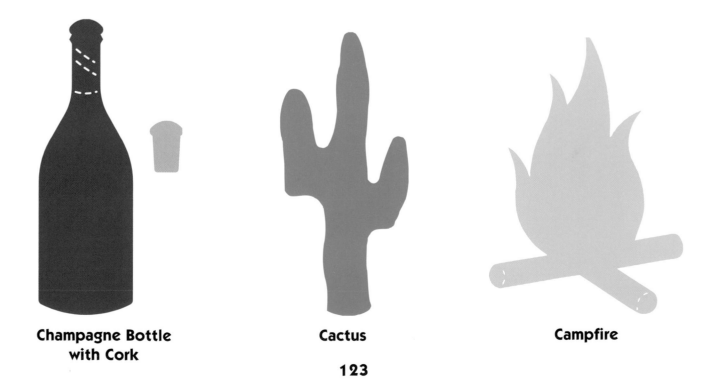

Border, Teddys

**Champagne Bottle
with Cork**

Cactus

Campfire

Canoe

Caption Boxes

Car #2

Cardinal

Cat #1

Chili Pepper

Christmas Light

Christmas Ornament #1B

Christmas Ornament #2B

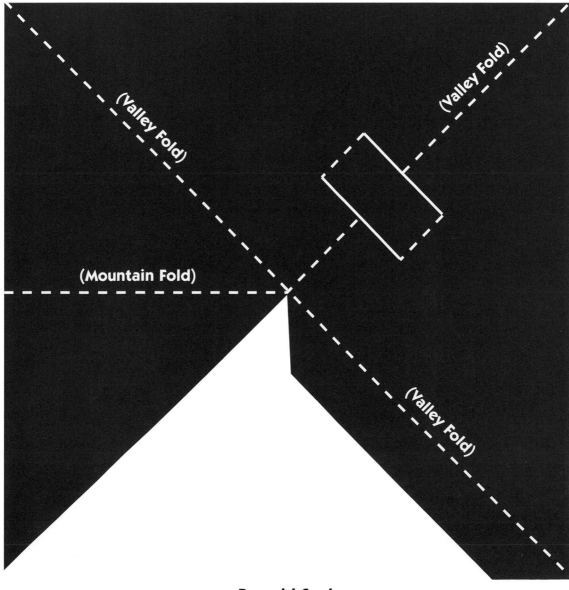

(Valley Fold)

(Valley Fold)

(Mountain Fold)

(Valley Fold)

Pyramid Card

125

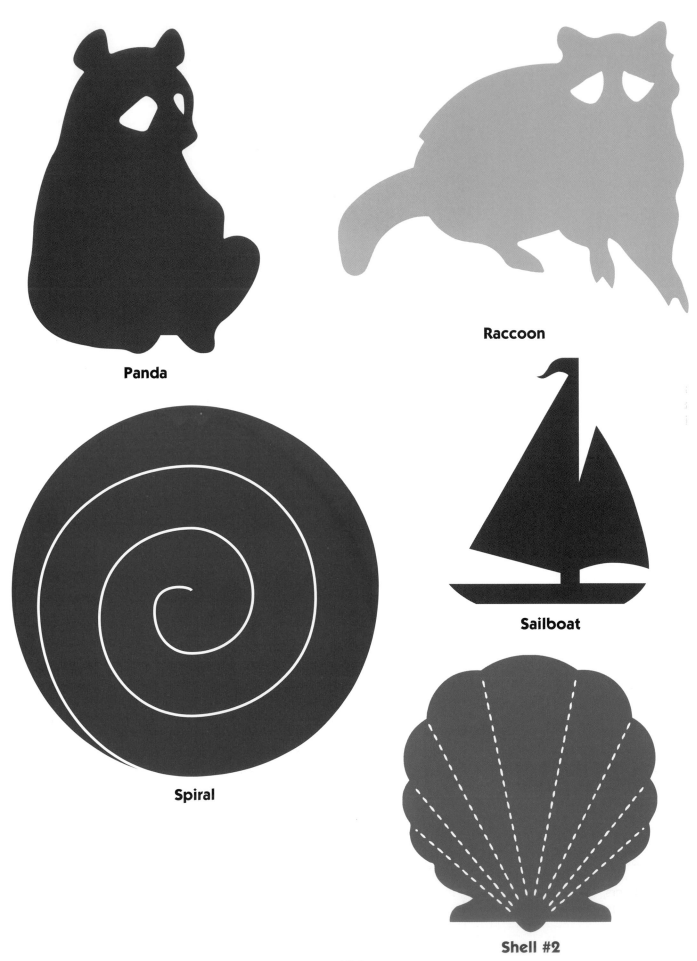

Panda

Raccoon

Sailboat

Spiral

Shell #2

126

Ellison Dies

Name	Stock No.
Bookmarks:	
Bookmark, Heart	B757HE
Borders:	
Border, Ivy	B770IV
Border, Mountain Range	B770MO
Decorative Dies:	
3-D Card, Plain	C17003
Accordion Card	A102
Accordion with Cutout	A103
Angel #1	AG51
Apple	A700
Balloons	B130
Bandage	B142
Banner	B143
Bath Tub	B160
Beach Ball	B294
Bird #2A	B572A
Bird #4	B574
Birthday Cake Slice	B582
Butterfly	B970
Candy #1	C164
Cat, Halloween	H150
Christmas Tree #2	C485
Clipboard	C520
Crayon	C725
Director Chair	D564
Duck, Toy	D891
Envelope, Open (2D)	E502
Filmstrip #1	F458
Filmstrip #2	F459
Ghost #2	G451
Gift Card with Insert	G445
Gift w/ Ribbon	G454
Guitar	G940
Hair Dryer	H140
Heart #1A	H315
Heart #1B	H310
Heart #2	H312
Heart, Primitive	H316
Holly	H770
Ladder	L049
Light, Spot	L525
Light Beam	L5626
Lips	L650
Mission	M555
Mitten	M560
Party Noisemaker #2	P176
Pencil	P345
Photo Corners, Decorative	P400
Photo Corners, Plain	P401
Pine Cone	P568
Pitcher	P585

Name	Stock No.
Pop-Up #1B	P811
Pumpkin #1A	P899
Pumpkin #1B	P900
School Bus Back	S242
Scissors	S251
Seed Packet	S320
Skier	S442
Square	GE402
Stars, Primitive (2 Up)	S817
Stethoscope	S855
Sunglasses	S903
Toothpaste	T658
Toothbrush & Tooth	T660
Triangle	GE400
Whale	W400
Dioramas:	
Front/Umbrellas	D56012
Middle/Flowers	D56009
Middle/Waves	D56013
Floral Dies:	
Anthurium	F56501
Bird of Paradise	F56502
Bluebonnet	B670
Daisy	D150
Iris	F56504
Rose	F56506
Sunflower	F56508
Tulip	T990
Music Dies:	
Musical Notes MX	M100
Summer Dies:	
Fish Hook	F479
Hawaiian Lei	H187
Palm Tree #2	P151
Pop-Up, Multiple	P800
Road Sign, Country	R700
Row Boat	R770
Snorkel & Mask	S457
Water Splash	W158
Tiny Dies:	
Apples, Tiny	A702
Balloons, Tiny	B131
Butterflies, Tiny	B971
Flowers, Tiny	F564
Hearts, Tiny	H320
Leaves, Tiny	L301
Words, Handwritten:	
"Birthday"	W900
"Congrats"	W902
"Happy"	W905
"Love"	W923
"Thanks"	W910

Metric Equivalency Chart

cm—Centimetres
Inches to Centimetres

inches	cm	inches	cm	inches	cm	inches	cm
⅛	.0.3	5	.12.7	21	.53.3	38	.96.5
¼	.0.6	6	.15.2	22	.55.9	39	.99.1
½	.1.3	7	.17.8	23	.58.4	40	.101.6
⅝	.1.6	8	.20.3	24	.61.0	41	.104.1
¾	.1.9	9	.22.9	25	.63.5	42	.106.7
⅞	.2.2	10	.25.4	26	.66.0	43	.109.2
1	.2.5	11	.27.9	27	.68.6	44	.111.8
1¼	.3.2	12	.30.5	28	.71.1	45	.114.3
1½	.3.8	13	.33.0	29	.73.7	46	.116.8
1¾	.4.4	14	.35.6	30	.76.2	47	.119.4
2	.5.1	15	.38.1	31	.78.7	48	.121.9
2½	.6.4	16	.40.6	33	.83.8	49	.124.5
3	.7.6	17	.43.2	34	.86.4	50	.127.0
3½	.8.9	18	.45.7	35	.88.9		
4	.10.2	19	.48.3	36	.91.4		
4½	.11.4	20	.50.8	37	.94.0		

Index

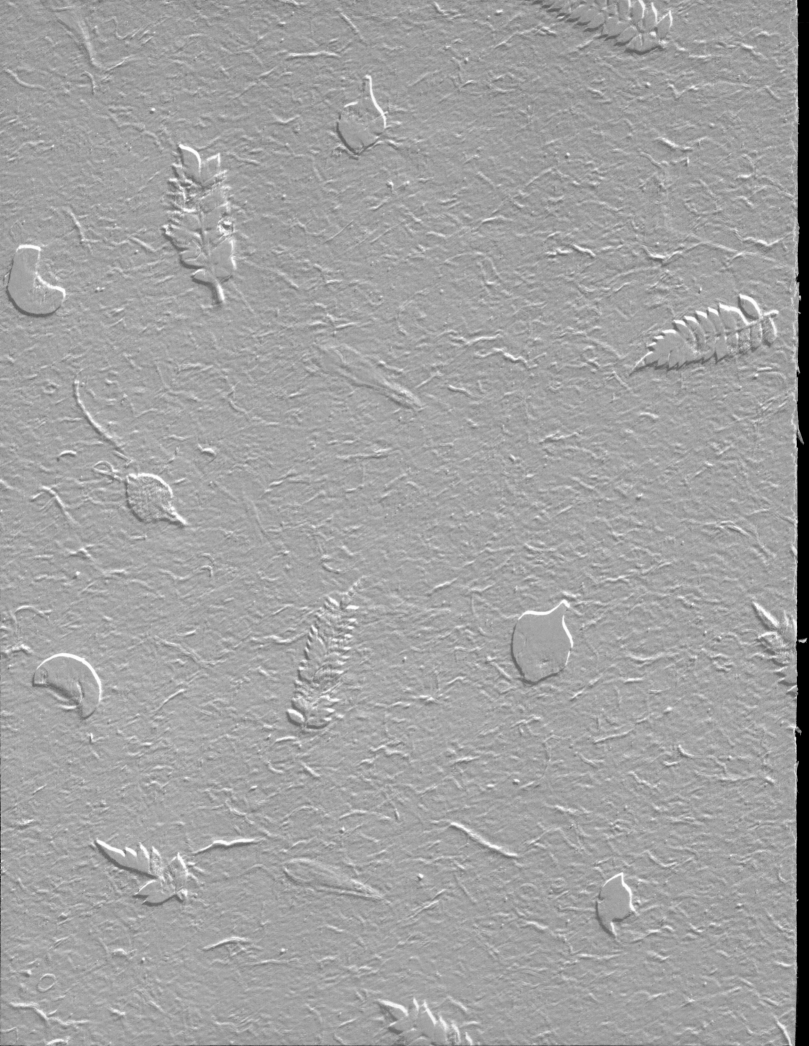